REGULATION
and TAXATION
of SHORT-TERM
RENTALS
Rebecca L. Badgett
Christopher B. McLaughlin

Publication Update

Short-Term Rental Regulations after *Schroeder v. City of Wilmington*, 282 N.C. App. 558 (2022).

Regulation and Taxation of Short-Term Rentals was published prior to the North Carolina Court of Appeals decision in *Schroeder v. City of Wilmington*, 282 N.C. App. 558 (2022). *Schroeder* is noteworthy because it is the first case in North Carolina to consider a local government's authority to regulate short-term rentals (STRs) as a separate land use. While this update provides a summary of the *Schroeder* decision and its impacts, a more-detailed analysis is available online through the UNC School of Government Coates' Canons Local Government Law Blog.[1]

1. Adam Lovelady, *Short-Term Rental Regulations after Schroeder*, Coates' Canons Loc. Gov't L. Blog (Apr. 14, 2022), https://canons.sog.unc.edu/2022/04/short-term-rental-regulations-after-schroeder/.

Case Overview

In early 2019, the City of Wilmington adopted an ordinance regulating short-term whole-house lodging. The ordinance authorized STRs in specified zoning districts subject to cap and separation requirements (2 percent cap and 400-foot separation between uses). The ordinance also required property owners to register their rental properties with the city. The city held a lottery to enforce the new regulations, and those who were not awarded a registration through the lottery process had a one-year amortization period to cease operations.

The Schroeders filed suit against the City of Wilmington to challenge the ordinance's registration requirement on the basis that state law preempted the city from requiring owners of rental property to register with the city. The outcome of the case depended on the court's interpretation of the state law relating to housing code inspections, permits, and registration programs. In 2019, the periodic inspection statutes, originally codified at G.S. 160A-424 and G.S. 153A-364, were consolidated into a single statutory provision, G.S. 160D-1207. During the recodification process, the legislature added the phrase "under Article 11 or Article 12 of this Chapter" to G.S. 160D-1207(c). The statute now provides:

> In no event may a local government . . . adopt or enforce any ordinance that would require any owner or manager of rental property to obtain any permit or permission <u>under Article 11 or Article 12 of this Chapter</u> from the local government to lease or rent residential real property or to register rental property with the local government . . .

On appeal, the City of Wilmington argued that the legislative intent in amending the statute during the recodification was to clarify that the restriction on registration programs was limited to Article 11 (the Minimum Housing Code) and Article 12 (the Building Code), and, therefore, a registration program implemented under Article 7 (zoning), like Wilmington's, would be permissible.

Appellate Court Decision

The Court of Appeals heard the case in *Schroeder v. City of Wilmington*, 282 N.C. App 558 (2022). The court was not persuaded by the City of Wilmington's argument, and it instead interpreted the limit on registrations broadly—meaning registration programs were not limited to housing code or building code enforcement under Articles 11 and 12. Accordingly, the court affirmed the trial court's decision that the registration provisions were invalid under G.S. 160D-1207(c) and struck down the registration requirement as being preempted by state law. In doing so, the court also struck down other ordinance provisions inextricably linked to the registration requirement, including the lottery, the 2 percent cap, the 400-foot separation requirement, and the one-year amortization period.

Importantly, the court did not strike down the entire short-term rental ordinance. Instead, the court invoked the ordinance's severance clause and affirmed several requirements unaffected by preemption, including restricting whole-house lodging to certain zoning districts; parking requirements (one off-street space per bedroom); prohibition on variances; operation limits and requirements (no large events, maintain insurance, manage trash, no food prep in bedrooms); posted safety information; and a few other use and safety requirements.

Schroeder's Impacts

Schroeder unmistakably affirmed that a local government in North Carolina may not require owners of rental property, including short-term rentals, to register with the local government as a condition of renting a property.

Further, by allowing certain provisions of the Wilmington ordinance to stand, the court affirmed that a local government has the authority to regulate short-term rentals as a separate land use and to adopt reasonable operational regulations. As such, a local government may likely require zoning-compliance permits and enforce regulations that promote the safety and welfare of the community. Such regulations may possibly include some of the provisions struck down in *Schroeder* (e.g., cap, separation requirement, lottery, and amortization period), as these regulations were possibly invalidated only because they were inextricably linked to the unlawful registration program. Certainly, any local government planning to issue zoning-compliance permits as part of the regulatory process should try to ensure that the permitting scheme does not resemble an unlawful rental registry. How to do this is not entirely clear. For starters, local governments will want to ensure that the issuance of any zoning permit is tied to compliance with reasonable zoning regulations. A local government may not simply collect the name and address of these properties.

REGULATION and TAXATION of SHORT-TERM RENTALS

Rebecca L. Badgett
Christopher B. McLaughlin

UNC SCHOOL OF GOVERNMENT

The School of Government at the University of North Carolina at Chapel Hill works to improve the lives of North Carolinians by engaging in practical scholarship that helps public officials and citizens understand and improve state and local government. Established in 1931 as the Institute of Government, the School provides educational, advisory, and research services for state and local governments. The School of Government is also home to a nationally ranked Master of Public Administration program, the North Carolina Judicial College, and specialized centers focused on community and economic development, information technology, and environmental finance.

As the largest university-based local government training, advisory, and research organization in the United States, the School of Government offers up to 200 courses, webinars, and specialized conferences for more than 12,000 public officials each year. In addition, faculty members annually publish approximately 50 books, manuals, reports, articles, bulletins, and other print and online content related to state and local government. The School also produces the *Daily Bulletin Online* each day the General Assembly is in session, reporting on activities for members of the legislature and others who need to follow the course of legislation.

Operating support for the School of Government's programs and activities comes from many sources, including state appropriations, local government membership dues, private contributions, publication sales, course fees, and service contracts.

Visit sog.unc.edu or call 919.966.5381 for more information on the School's courses, publications, programs, and services.

Printed in the United States of America

27 26 25 24 23 2 3 4 5 6

ISBN 978-1-56011-950-0

Contents

Introduction

The concept of the short-term vacation rental is not a new one. It has had a place in history for some time now. The earliest record of vacation homes dates back to the mid-1600s, the first one being Louis XIV's hunting lodge at the Palace of Versailles.[1] In the 1950s, vacation rentals began to appear in the United States and were advertised in local newspapers.[2] By 1969, the first condominium timeshare was built in Kauai, Hawaii. In 1985, a gathering of vacation rental managers in Monterey, California, resulted in the formation of the Vacation Rental Management Association (VRMA), an international association that offers networking and professional development opportunities to its members "to advance the vacation rental industry."[3] In 1995, the first vacation rental site was listed on the Internet, Vacation Rental by Owner (VRBO).[4] Short-term rentals (STRs) hit their stride in the sharing economy[5] by the mid-to-late 2000s, when web-based companies, such as Airbnb, HomeAway, and FlipKey, followed VRBO's example and began marketing vacation properties directly to consumers.

The growth in this sector of the sharing economy may be attributable to increased autonomy in the booking of vacation homes, or perhaps it is due to the feeling of "living like a local." Whatever the reason, travelers are smitten with the concept of STRs and property owners enjoy having an additional income source, so these types of rentals seem to be here to stay.

In light of a documented global demand for STRs, the question of how to regulate these properties has become a key issue for local governments. The regulation of STRs is controversial, to put it mildly. It requires local governments to weigh

---

1. Ife Ankande, *The History of Vacation Rentals – Infographic*, RENTALS UNITED blog (Oct. 20, 2015), https://rentalsunited.com/blog/history-of-vacation-rentals-infographic/.

2. *Id.*

3. VRMA, *About the Vacation Rental Management Association*, VRMA.ORG, http://www.vrma.org/page/about-vrma.

4. Crunchbase, *Overview*, CRUNCHBASE.COM, https://www.crunchbase.com/organization/vrbo#section-overview (listing 1995 as the year of VRBO's founding).

5. The term *sharing economy* is commonly used to describe peer-to-peer–based consumption and the shared access to goods and services. *See* Thomas S. Walker, *Searching for the Right Approach: Regulating Short-Term Rentals in North Carolina*, 96 N.C. L. REV. 1831, 1824 (2017) ("sharing economy" refers to an "economic model where people are creating and sharing goods, services, space and money with each other").

the rights inherent in property ownership against the rights of individuals and businesses claiming that STRs are disrupting communities and contributing to an affordable housing crisis. This is a difficult balancing act.

The purpose of this publication is twofold. The first part is dedicated to exploring ways in which local governments may regulate STRs in North Carolina. The second part discusses the intricacies of the occupancy tax and explores the intersection of this tax and short-term rentals. The occupancy tax is a separate tax levied on the rental of an accommodation. Today, more than 150 North Carolina counties and municipalities levy a local occupancy tax.[6] This tax is an important tool for promoting local growth by generating billions in tax revenue that flows directly back to a state's or local government's tourist economy.

And the revenue generated by this tax only continues to grow. In 2016, North Carolina welcomed nearly 50 million visitors, making it America's sixth most-visited state, behind only California, Florida, Texas, New York, and Pennsylvania.[7]

The School of Government at the University of North Carolina at Chapel Hill offers the guidance contained herein with the following caveat: The law governing short-term rentals is still developing and changing, both within North Carolina and across the nation. There are no settled "best practices" for regulating these types of properties.[8] Each local government should consult with its counsel and other members of pertinent advisory boards to decide whether and how to regulate STRs in light of specific community needs.

---

6. N.C. Gen. Assemb., Research Div., Occupancy Tax Overview (updated through 2018 Reg. Sess.), https://canons.sog.unc.edu/wp-content/uploads/2013/11/OCCUPANCY-TAX-OVERVIEW-TABLE-2018.pdf. This document lists the local bills, rates, and restrictions on the use of proceeds for each jurisdiction in North Carolina that levies occupancy taxes.

7. *See* N.C. Travel & Tourism Coal. (NCTTC), *About*, NCTTC.com, http://www.ncttc.com/about.

8. *See, e.g.*, City of Wilmington, N.C., Land Development Code Amendment p. 4 (Dec. 6, 2017), https://www.wilmingtonnc.gov/home/showdocument?id=6760 ("there are no clear best practices or standards for addressing the issue of peer-to-peer rentals").

I. "Short-Term Rental" Defined

A *short-term rental* (STR) is the rental of a residence (or part thereof) to a transient lodger for a limited duration, usually thirty days or fewer.[9] There are two key parties to an STR transaction: the *host* and the *guest*.[10] The host is the property owner (or, sometimes, leaseholder) who advertises the property for rent.[11] The guest is the tourist or business traveler who books the rental and stays overnight in the accommodation. A *hosting platform* or *STR platform* is an online entity that facilitates, through advertising or other means, booking transactions for accommodations between hosts and guests, including by allowing for reservations to be made by guests and for payments to be collected on behalf of hosts.

There are two common STR models. The first is a *home-sharing model* (often called a "homestay" STR), where the guest and host are co-occupants of a dwelling unit being used as a short-term rental. In this situation, the host remains on-site during the rental period. The second is a simple *short-term rental model* (sometimes called a "whole-house" STR), where the entire dwelling unit is rented while the host is away from the property.

A few cities outside of North Carolina distinguish between *owner-occupied* and *not-owner-occupied* STRs. In an owner-occupied STR, the dwelling being rented is the host's primary residence, while in a not-owner-occupied STR, the rental dwelling has no primary resident and is likely rented on a regular basis. Jurisdictions in North Carolina may want to choose regulatory terms that are less focused on owner occupation. If the goal is to require a host to reside on-site, consider using the term "resident-occupied" or "on-site residence."[12] It is common for homestays to be regulated differently (often less restrictively) than whole-house STRs owing

---

9. *See, e.g.*, Blowing Rock, N.C., Town Code, Land Use Ordinance § 16-2.2, http://www.townofblowingrocknc.gov/home/showdocument?id=244 (defining "Short-Term Rental of a Dwelling Unit" as "[t]he rental, lease, or use of an attached or detached residential dwelling unit for a duration that is less than 28 consecutive days").

10. Cory Scanlon, *Re-zoning the Sharing Economy: Municipal Authority to Regulate Short-Term Rentals of Real Property*, 70 SMU L. Rev. 563, 567 (2017), https://scholar.smu.edu/cgi/viewcontent.cgi?article=4691&context=smulr (recognizing that the "host" and "guest" are key parties in the rental transaction but also considering the "platform" to be a key party). "Platform," in the context of STRs, is defined in the text below.

11. In this publication the terms "host" and "owner" are used interchangeably.

12. North Carolina case law is clear that the *use* of property may be regulated but its *ownership* may not. In drafting an STR ordinance, a local government may want to be mindful not to use terms that suggest ownership is being regulated. *See* City of Wilmington v. Hill, 189 N.C. App. 173 (2008); Graham Ct. Assocs. v. Town of Chapel Hill, 53 N.C. App. 543 (1981).

Figure 1. Snapshot: U.S. STR Listings, by Share of Market and Platform

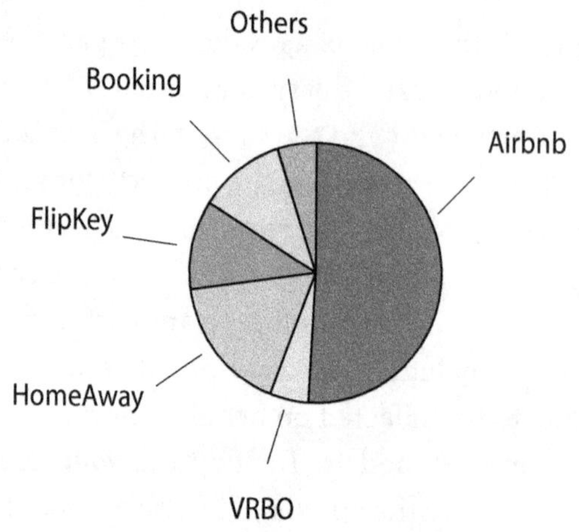

Source: "Airbnb Dominates the Short-Term Rental Business," *in* Paris Martineau, *Inside Airbnb's "Guerilla War" Against Local Governments*, WIRED (Mar. 20,2019), https://www.wired.com/story/inside-airbnbs-guerrilla-war-against-local-governments/amp.

to the fact that these properties, by definition, are resident-/owner-occupied.[13] This publication primarily addresses the regulation of whole-house STRs, which will be referred to as "short-term rentals" or "STRs" from here on in. However, should a jurisdiction want to separately regulate homestays, many of the suggested regulations discussed herein would also apply.

As mentioned above, an STR platform is an online company that connects hosts to guests.[14] Although there are numerous STR platforms, each catering to a different niche or demographic, a few sites dominate this market, including Airbnb, VRBO, HomeAway, and TripAdvisor Vacation Rentals.

Airbnb is likely the most recognized STR platform. The site was started in the late 2000s to entice adventurous, budget-conscious travelers to embrace the home-sharing model in metropolitan cities.[15] The platform now has between 4 and

---

13. *See* CITY OF ASHEVILLE, N.C., CODE OF ORDINANCES §§ 7-8-1(d) (permitted use table) (homestays are allowed as a permitted use in residential districts, while STRs are not), https://library.municode.com/nc/asheville/codes/code_of_ordinances?nodeId=PTIICOOR_CH7DE_ARTVIIIGEUSEXDI_S7-8-1ENDEDIDEDIOFZOMA; 7-2-5 (defining "homestay" and "short-term vacation rental"), https://library.municode.com/nc/asheville/codes/code_of_ordinances?nodeId=PTIICOOR_CH7DE_ARTIIOFMARUCODE_S7-2-5DE.

14. *See* Scanlon, *supra* note 10.

15. Airbnb was first called Air Bed and Breakfast, and the company initially focused on the idea of renting air mattresses within other people's apartments. To help launch the company, the founders visited—and stayed with—all the hosts in New York City, writing reviews and photographing the rental spaces in the process. Biz Carson,

5 million global listings.[16] The company promotes the notion of an authentic travel experience, a concept that has been bolstered by its global branding campaign, "Live There."[17] In addition to lodging, Airbnb has released a "trips" feature that allows customers to purchase experience packages at their destinations. According to CEO Brian Chesky, "the number one reason people chose to travel on Airbnb is they want to live like a local."[18] Apparently Chesky is on to something—the company is currently valued at approximately $38 billion.[19]

HomeAway is another leading platform for vacation rentals, with more than 2 million STR listings in 190 countries.[20] The company gained its market share by slowly acquiring more than twenty competing vacation rental sites, including VRBO (in 2006) and VacationRentals.com (in 2007).[21] In 2015, Expedia purchased HomeAway and all of its global brands for $3.9 billion.[22] HomeAway is unique in that it offers property owners the choice between a subscription model or a pay-per-booking model.

TripAdvisor Vacation Rentals delved into the STR market in 2008, when it acquired the popular STR platform FlipKey. Just two years later it purchased Holiday Lettings, the UK's largest vacation rental site at the time, followed by Spain's leading STR site, Niumba, in 2013, and then the Massachusetts-based Vacation

---

How 3 Guys Turned Renting an Air Mattress in Their Apartment into a $25 Billion Company, BUSINESS INSIDER (Feb. 23, 2016), https://www.businessinsider.com/how-airbnb-was-founded-a-visual-history-2016-2.

16. *As Rare Profitable Unicorn, Airbnb Appears to Be Worth at Least $38 Billion*, FORBES (May 11, 2018), https://www.forbes.com/sites/greatspeculations/2018/05/11/as-a-rare-profitable-unicorn-airbnb-appears-to-be-worth-at-least-38-billion/#44b50f4e2741.

17. *Airbnb Launches New Products to Inspire People to "Live There,"* BUSINESS WIRE (Apr. 19, 2016), https://www.businesswire.com/news/home/20160419006571/en/Airbnb-Launches-Products-Inspire-People-%E2%80%9CLive-There%E2%80%9D.

18. *Id.*

19. FORBES, *supra* note 16.

20. HomeAway, *What you get*, HOMEAWAY.COM, https://www.homeaway.com/lp/learn-more/.

21. Peter Lane Taylor, *Watch Out, HomeAway and Airbnb: Here's Why TripAdvisor May Be Your Biggest Competition*, FORBES (Dec. 7, 2016), https://www.forbes.com/sites/petertaylor/2016/12/07/watch-out-homeaway-airbnb-heres-why-tripadvisor-may-be-your-biggest-competition/#1a837d4a736d ("HomeAway's business model has been surprisingly simplistic: growth and superiority through acquisition. Since its founding in 2005, HomeAway has snatched up over 20 other vacation rental sites, consolidating them under a single technology platform.").

22. Leslie Picker, *Expedia to Acquire HomeAway for $3.9 Billion*, N.Y. TIMES (Nov. 4, 2015), https://www.nytimes.com/2015/11/05/business/dealbook/expedia-to-acquire-homeaway-for-3-9-billion.html.

Home Rentals in 2014.[23] TripAdvisor now offers STRs in more than 200 countries.[24] Its increasing popularity among travelers is likely due in part to the fact that the platform acts as a one-stop-shop for travel needs—travelers can rent a property, book flights, rent cars, and read reviews for local restaurants, all without opening another website.[25]

Traditional brick and mortar property rental companies in North Carolina have increasingly begun to advertise vacation rentals on STR platforms or have adopted a rental model that mirrors the web-based rental platforms. For example, a few property rental companies have scratched the traditional week-long rental period in favor of allowing stays of a shorter duration.[26]

II. Local Authority to Regulate Short-Term Rentals

In North Carolina, local governments are vested with authority to regulate the use of real property, including residences, through zoning and development regulation ordinances.[27] Zoning regulations constitute a proper exercise of the government's police power and thus enjoy a strong presumption of validity if they serve a public purpose related to the "public health, safety, morals, or general welfare" of the communities they regulate.[28] The power to zone "is subject to the limitations imposed by the Constitution upon the legislative power forbidding arbitrary and unduly discriminatory interference with the rights of property owners."[29] Thus, local governments may not enact "unreasonable and confiscatory" property regu-

---

23. Taylor, *supra* note 21.

24. TripAdvisor, *Vacation Rentals*, TRIPADVISOR.COM, https://www.tripadvisor.com/Rentals.

25. Taylor, *supra* note 21.

26. Village Realty, located on North Carolina's Outer Banks, prominently advertises on its website the fact that it allows "stays of just three nights in many of [its rental] homes." Village Realty, *Partial Week or Short Stay Rentals*, VILLAGEREALTYOBX.COM, https://www.villagerealtyobx.com/outer-banks-vacation-rentals/partial-week-or-short-stay#q=im_nid%24field_vr_amenities_top%3A660.

27. Chapter 153A, Section 340 of the North Carolina General Statutes (hereinafter G.S.) ("For the purpose of promoting health, safety, morals, or the general welfare, a county may adopt zoning and development regulation ordinances"); *id.* § 160A-381 (same for cities).

28. City of Wilmington v. Hill, 189 N.C. App. 173, 177 (2008) ("zoning ordinance will be declared invalid only where the record demonstrates that it has no foundation in reason and bears no substantial relation to the public health, the public morals, the public safety or the public welfare in its proper sense").

29. Zopfi v. City of Wilmington, 273 N.C. 430, 434 (1968).

lations under the "guise of the police power."[30] If there is a question as to the interpretation of a zoning ordinance, the ordinance is to be "liberally construed in favor of freedom of use."[31] Several jurisdictions in North Carolina have enacted local ordinances governing short-term rentals (STRs), and it is reasonable to think that local governments are vested with authority to regulate these properties, just as they may regulate hotels, motels, boarding houses, and bed and breakfasts (B&Bs).

A. Zoning to Regulate Location of Short-Term Rentals

A local government may use its zoning authority to regulate the areas in which STRs lawfully operate. In doing so, it may be helpful to regulate whole-house STRs and homestays separately, as each has a different potential land-use impact. In a homestay, the owner or permanent resident remains on-site throughout the entire rental period, making the stay more akin to that of a visiting house guest. Accordingly, most jurisdictions that regulate STRs allow homestays to operate in residential zoning districts.[32] This is likely because there is a limited land-use impact associated with homestays—the neighborhood retains its residential feel.

A few jurisdictions, particularly in densely populated cities, are considering or have adopted regulations to exclude or limit the number of whole-house STRs operating in residential zoning districts. The reason for this is a belief that the land-use impacts of STRs are inconsistent with the residential use of property. Whole-house STRs arguably change the character of a neighborhood and contribute to affordable housing issues. For these reasons, some jurisdictions prefer to limit STRs to commercial and mixed-use zoning districts, as they contend that this land use is more closely associated with that of hotels and other types of transient accommodations. Asheville, N.C., is one city that has relied heavily on its zoning authority to greatly restrict the areas in which whole-house STRs may lawfully operate. These properties are presently allowed, subject to special standards, in the city's Resort District and are permitted by right in the Central Business Expansion District,

30. Vill. of Euclid v. Ambler Realty Co., 272 U.S. 365, 387 (1926).

31. Application of Rea Constr. Co., 272 N.C. 715, 718 (1968).

32. The city of Asheville, N.C., allows homestays to operate in residential zoning districts provided that hosts obtain a homestay permit. *Asheville's Homestay and Short-Term Rental Regulation Program Processing*, Asheville City Source, official blog for the City of Asheville, N.C. (July 13, 2016), http://coablog.ashevillenc.gov/2016/07/ashevilles-homestay-and-short-term-rental-regulation-program-progressing/.

Lodging Expansion District, and Mixed-Use Expansion District.[33] The city has banned STRs from all other zoning districts, including residential neighborhoods.[34]

A complete ban of STRs may prove problematic for a local government. There is a general belief that all lawful land uses should be permitted somewhere within a jurisdiction's boundaries. But the question of whether every jurisdiction is *required to make space available* for all lawful land uses has not yet been resolved in North Carolina's courts.[35] Most lawful land uses typically have a place within every jurisdiction, and a variety of land uses have even been afforded either constitutional or statutory protection that prevents their total exclusion.[36] Local governments should give much thought and care to any decision to completely exclude a particular land use. While it may be tempting to ban any controversial use of property, this should be done only after a thorough investigation of the impacts of such a ban on use.[37] A complete prohibition of STRs within all zoning districts of a local government unit may be found to be an arbitrary and capricious land-use regulation.

This section is not meant to suggest that whole-house STRs should necessarily be restricted to certain commercial or mixed-use zoning districts. In fact, doing so may not be desirable for some communities that rely heavily on tourism to promote the local economy. For example, the homes in most beach towns are zoned for res-

---

33. Asheville, N.C., Code of Ordinances § 7-8-1(d) (permitted use table), https://library.municode.com/nc/asheville/codes/code_of_ordinances?nodeId=PTIICOOR_CH7DE_ARTVIIIGEUSEXDI_S7-8-1ENDEDIDEDIOFZOMA.

34. Asheville allows homestays in all zoning districts.

35. David W. Owens, *Does Zoning Have to Provide a Place for Everything?*, Coates' Canons: NC Loc. Gov't L. blog (May 10, 2010), https://www.sog.unc.edu/blogs/coates-canons/does-zoning-have-provide-place-everything. Other states have expressed skepticism regarding the constitutionality of zoning ordinances that totally prohibit legitimate land uses and businesses. *See, e.g.*, Kropf v. City of Sterling Heights, 391 Mich. 139, 155–56 (1974) ("On its face, an ordinance which totally excludes from a municipality a use recognized by the Constitution or other laws of this state as legitimate also carries with it a strong taint of unlawful discrimination and a denial of equal protection of the law as to the excluded use"); Exton Quarries, Inc. v. Zoning Bd. of Adjustment, 425 Pa. 43, 59 (1967) (striking down ordinance totally banning quarries where there was no showing of harmful effects and holding that "[t]he constitutionality of zoning ordinances which totally prohibit legitimate businesses such as quarrying from an entire community should be regarded with particular circumspection").

36. *See* Owens, *supra* note 35 ("Other uses with statutory protection include family care homes in residential districts, facilities with a state ABC license, and bona fide farm uses in county jurisdiction. Federal statutes protect a few uses as well, such as prohibiting a total ban on wireless telecommunication towers. Other uses have constitutional protection. Courts have held, for example, that a total prohibition of non-obscene adult entertainment would violate First Amendment free speech rights.").

37. *Id.* ("Total exclusion of a particular land use is a powerful tool that should be applied quite carefully.").

idential use, and the local economy would suffer if none of these homes could be rented on a short-term basis. Therefore, it is important for local officials to consider the ramifications of banning STRs from certain zoning districts.

B. Registration Programs for Short-Term Rentals

It is likely lawful to require a host to register with the local government any short-term rental property he or she owns. Nationally, most cities that regulate STRs issue STR permits. Local governments in North Carolina may rely on their zoning authority to regulate STRs, specifically, both county and municipal zoning officials are vested with statutory authority to inspect property, receive applications for zoning permits, and grant an issuance or denial thereof.[38] Within our state, Blowing Rock, Asheville, and Lake Lure issue short-term rental zoning permits to hosts.[39] Lake Lure calls its permit a "Vacation Rental Operating Permit." On the face of the application for this permit, it is clear that it is an application for a certificate of zoning compliance. One benefit to requiring STR permits is that it allows these properties to be more identifiable, making it easier to enforce regulations and collect taxes.

There has been some question as to whether local governments are statutorily prohibited from requiring the registration of STRs due to the Periodic Inspections for Hazardous or Unlawful Conditions statutes, G.S. 153A-364 (counties) and 160A-424 (cities). These statutes expressly prohibit a local government from adopting an ordinance mandating that a property owner obtain a permit or permission to do any one of the following: (1) lease residential property, (2) register a rental property, or (3) "levy a special fee or tax on residential rental property that is not also levied against other commercial and residential properties."[40] While these laws appear at first glance to disallow STR registration and the imposition of fees associated therewith, this is not necessarily the case. The statutes' titles and the provisions contained therein suggest that they were enacted to protect owners

---

38. *See* G.S. 160A-411, -412 (cities); 153A-351, -352 (counties) (authorizing zoning officials to undertake such activities).

39. Asheville, N.C., Code § 7-5-2(c), https://library.municode.com/nc/asheville/codes/code_of_ordinances?nodeId=PTIICOOR_CH7DE_ARTVDEREPR_S7-5-2ZOPE; Blowing Rock, N.C., Town Code, Land Use Ordinance § 16.10.12 (Note: Blowing Rock has adopted an STR ordinance and plans to start enforcement of it in spring 2019; the authors have a draft of adopted regulations for Blowing Rock, including the one cited here, on file); Lake Lure, N.C., Code § 92.042(A), https://www.egovlink.com/public_documents300/lakelure/published_documents/Town%20Ordinances/Chapter_92_Zoning_Regulations.pdf.

40. G.S. 153A-364(c), 160A-424(c).

and landlords of long-term rental property from arbitrary safety inspections, property registration requirements, and/or special fees that were not similarly imposed on other property owners. These statutes make no reference to short-term rental properties. One way to frame this issue is to ask the following questions: When someone stays at an Airbnb, is that person a tenant? Is the operator a landlord? Property rental websites frequently use the terms "host" and "guest," both of which are associated with lodging. Thus, the practice of short-term rentals seems closer to the type of transient tenancy associated with the hospitality business, not with residential tenancy. This is further evidenced by the fact that hosts must pay occupancy taxes on the income derived from rental stays. Although future interpretation of these statutes could render certain regulatory actions unlawful, for now, it is unlikely that these statutes prohibit local governments from requiring STR hosts to register short-term rental properties.

C. Registration Fees

Fees are often assessed to cover the costs associated with administering the regulatory activities performed by counties and municipalities, such as issuing zoning permits and enforcing local ordinances.[41] Thus, local governments may "fix reasonable fees for issuing permits, for inspections, and for other services of the inspection department."[42] The revenue generated from these fees must be used to "support . . . the administration and activities of the inspection department and for no other purpose."[43] Counties have additional statutory authority to allow boards of commissioners to set reasonable fees and charges for services performed by county officers and employees.[44] This provision likely vests in county boards the authority to charge fees for other kinds of regulatory activity. There is no analogous statute for counties. However, in *Homebuilders Ass'n of Charlotte, Inc. v. City of Charlotte,* the North Carolina Supreme Court held that the authority to operate a regulatory program generally also implies the power to impose reasonable fees to support its operation.[45] There is one caveat—the regulatory fees charged must

---

41. Kara A. Millonzi, *Revenue Sources, in* Introduction to Local Government Finance, 78 (Kara A. Millonzi ed., 4th ed., 2018).

42. G.S. 153A-354(a) (counties); 160A-414(a) (cities)

43. G.S. 153A-354(c) (counties); 160A-414(c) (cities).

44. G.S. 153A-102; *see also* Millonzi, *supra* note 41.

45. 336 N.C. 37, 42 (1994) ("The generally accepted rule today seems to be that the municipal power to regulate an activity implies the power to impose a fee in an amount sufficient to cover the cost of regulation.").

Quiz: Administrative Fees

Facts: A city determines that the cost of properly administering a short-term-rental regulatory program will work out to $108 per program applicant. One local official suggests that the city charge $150 per applicant and use the additional funds to improve the downtown tourist area. May the local government charge applicants $150?

Answer: No. Local officials may not charge fees that exceed the costs of administering the regulatory activities at issue.

be reasonable, meaning the local government may not charge fees that exceed the costs of funding the regulatory activities.[46] No profit may be made from the regulatory fees.

Local governments will have to calculate the costs of running an STR licensing program to ensure that any associated application and renewal fees do not exceed the administrative costs of the program. The fees charged for STR licenses vary considerably nationwide. Asheville, N.C., requires applicants for homestay permits to pay a $208 registration and technology fee.[47] Savannah, Ga., requires applicants to pay a $300 initial application fee, with a $150 annual renewal fee imposed thereafter.[48] Denver, Colo., requires applicants to pay a $50 Lodger's Tax ID License fee every two years, plus an annual $25 business license fee.[49] San Francisco, Cal., requires license applicants pay a $250 non-refundable application fee.[50] Allowing for the online registration of STRs and for the payment of associated fees will likely increase compliance with any newly enacted business registration program.

---

46. Millonzi, *supra* note 41.

47. City of Asheville, N.C., Dev. Servs. Dep't, Homestay Application & Submittal Requirements, http://www.ashevillenc.gov/civicax/filebank/blobdload.aspx?BlobID=23416.

48. Savannah, Ga., Short-Term Rental Certificate Application, https://www.savannahga.gov/DocumentCenter/View/4690/STVR-Application.

49. Denver, Colo., *Short-Term Rental License Overview*, Denver.org https://www.denvergov.org/content/denvergov/en/denver-business-licensing-center/business-licenses/short-term-rentals.html (Short-Term Rental Application accessible by registering an account).

50. S.F. Bus. Portal, *Short-Term Residential Rental Starter Kit*, SFGov.org, https://businessportal.sfgov.org/start/starter-kits/short-term-rental (downloadable tool containing Guides, Related Documents, and Permits).

III. Approaches to Short-Term Rental Regulation

Within the past few years, a growing number of cities have enacted ordinances to regulate short-term rentals (STRs) by imposing safeguards that protect public interests.[51] The list of cities with robust regulatory frameworks includes Savannah, Ga.; Nashville, Tenn.; Austin, Tex.; San Francisco, Cal.; Seattle, Wash.; Columbus, Ohio; and Denver, Colo. Each of these cities has approached STR regulation differently in order to respond to local needs, meaning no two ordinances on the topic are the same. But there are similarities between the various provisions. When STRs are a permitted use within a jurisdiction, hosts are often asked to comply with local health and safety standards, to show proof of liability insurance, to designate an emergency contact, to affirm that their STRs do not violate homeowners association (HOA) bylaws, and to agree to abide by certain maximum occupancy requirements. Cities with affordable housing concerns sometimes limit or ban not-owner-occupied STRs from single-family or two-family zoning districts. The discussion below addresses how a few cities have approached STR regulation. Readers should bear in mind that some of these regulatory approaches may not be lawful in North Carolina.

A. Municipal Regulation Outside North Carolina

Austin, Tex., has a reputation for being among the most restrictive cities for STR use in the country. Under a city ordinance, Austin classifies STRs in one of three ways and issues licenses according to type: Type 1 is an owner-occupied principal residence, Type 2 is a not-owner-occupied single-family or duplex property; and Type 3 is a not-owner-occupied multifamily-use property.[52] The city has faced much backlash for its heavy regulation of STRs, particularly of Type 2 properties. Austin initially capped at 3 percent the number of homes within a census tract that could be issued a Type 2 STR license. It has now placed a moratorium on issuing new Type 2 licenses and plans to phase out Type 2 rentals in residential areas entirely by April 1, 2022.[53] Thus, Austin has effectively imposed a

---

51. Yassi Eskandari-QuJar & Janelle Orsi, Sustainable Econs. L. Ctr., Regulating Short-Term Rentals: A Guidebook for Equitable Policy 10 (Mar. 2016), available for download at https://www.theselc.org/regulating_short_term_rentals_a_guidebook_for_equitable_policy.

52. Austin Code Dep't, *Rental Types*, "Types of Short Term Rentals," AustinTexas.gov, https://www.austintexas.gov/page/rental-types.

53. Austin Code Dep't, *Short Term Rental News Release and FAQ*, "Austin Code Department Announces Details of New Short-Term Rental Ordinance" AustinTexas.gov (Mar. 17, 2016), http://austintexas.gov/article/short-term-rental-news-release-and-faq.

primary-residency requirement for single-family STRs located within a residential zoning district. The city has also capped at 3 percent the number of units within a multifamily property located within a non-commercial zoning district that may be issued a Type 3 STR license; for units within a multifamily dwelling located in a commercial district, that figure is raised to 25 percent.[54] The city has banned STR guests from hosting "commercial events" such as bachelor parties, weddings, or other large events.[55]

A challenge to the Austin STR ordinance is currently pending before the state's appellate court.[56] The case was filed by private plaintiffs who contend that the city's ban on the leasing of Type 2 rentals is unlawful.[57] The State of Texas intervened as a plaintiff in the action, asserting that the "ordinance violates the anti-retroactivity clause of the [state] constitution and [amounts to] an uncompensated taking of private property."[58] The City of Austin (appellee) contends that the ordinance is a valid exercise of the city's regulatory authority and substantially advances legitimate governmental purposes.[59] A final decision in this case is forthcoming.

Nashville, Tenn., offers two types of permits for STR properties: a "short term rental property (STRP)—owner occupied" permit or a "short term rental property (STRP)—not owner occupied" permit. The owner-occupied permit is for primary residents who wish to occasionally rent out their residences, while the not-owner-occupied permit is issued to property owners who operate full-time STRs. In Nashville, not-owner-occupied STRs are banned from single-family and two-family zoning districts. These properties are permitted uses (with conditions) in the city's multifamily, mixed-use, commercial, and downtown districts.[60] When applying for an STR permit, a prospective host must, among other things, (1) submit

---

54. Austin, Tex., Land Dev. Code § 25-2-791(C), https://library.municode.com/tx/austin/codes/land_development_code?nodeId=TIT25LADE_CH25-2ZO_SUBCHAPTER_CUSDERE_ART4ADRECEUS_SPCRESHRMREUS_S25-2-791LIRE.

55. Austin Code Dep't, *supra* note 52.

56. Zaatari v. City of Austin, *original petition filed with Tex. Judic. Dist. Ct.* (June 17, 2016), *appeal docketed*, No. 03-17-00812-cv (Tex. App. Mar. 29, 2018).

57. *See* Brief for Appellant State of Texas, *Zaatari* (No. 03-17-00812), 2018 WL 1718098, at *xvi (Tex. App. Mar. 29, 2018).

58. *Id. See also* Tex. Const. art. I, § 16 ("No bill of attainder, ex post facto law, retroactive law, or any law impairing the obligation of contracts, shall be made.").

59. *See* Brief for Appellee City of Austin, *Zaatari* (No. 03-17-00812), 2018 WL 2203570, at *12 (Tex. App. Apr. 30, 2018) ("The legislative record shows substantial public concern about issues of health, safety, general welfare, and neighborhood preservation. Under rational basis scrutiny, the 2016 ordinance substantially advances legitimate governmental purposes and survives challenge.").

60. Code of Metro. Gov't of Nashville & Davidson Cty., Tenn., § 17.08.030, https://library.municode.com/tn/metro_government_of_nashville_and_davidson_county/codes/code_of_ordinances?nodeId=CD_TIT17ZO_CH17.08ZODILAUS_17.08.030DILAUSTA.

a site plan, (2) show proof of liability insurance, (3) notify adjacent homeowners that his or her property is to be used as an STR, and (4) submit an HOA statement indicating that the STR will not violate any HOA agreement or bylaws.[61] The city also requires smoke alarms in STR properties and caps the occupancy of all STRs at no more than twice the number of sleeping rooms plus four, for a maximum of twelve.[62]

Savannah, Ga., allows owner-occupied STRs in most zoning districts but has implemented a 20-percent-per-ward cap on not-owner-occupied properties located in the city's residential or conservation wards within the boundaries of the Savannah Historic District.[63] The city requires any new applicant for a short-term vacation rental certificates to include with the application, among other things, (1) a "sworn code compliance verification form;" (2) proof of insurance indicating that the property is to be used as an STR; (3) a statement that the property owner agrees to "use his or her best efforts to assure that use of the premises by short-term vacation rental occupants will not disrupt the neighborhood, and will not interfere with the rights of neighboring property owners to the quiet enjoyment of their properties;" (4) the designation of an emergency contact person; and (5) a copy of an "exemplar rental agreement," required to be executed between the host and all guests, indicating certain operational restrictions for the property.[64] The city has capped the occupancy of STRs to no more than two adults per bedroom.[65]

The city of Columbus, Ohio, has taken a different, perhaps milder, approach to STR regulation. Like other cities, by ordinance Columbus requires proof of liability insurance, a designated emergency contact, the display of the STR permit number on all advertisements, and more.[66] However, Columbus does not distinguish between owner-occupied and not-owner-occupied rentals in terms of where they may be located within the city's zoning districts. This means that there is no primary residency requirement for STRs to operate in single-family residential zones.

---

61. Metro Gov't of Nashville & Davidson Cty., Tenn., Nashville Codes Administration, *Applying for a Short Term Rental Property Permit*, "Short Term Rental Permit Application Checklist," NASHVILLE.GOV, https://www.nashville.gov/Codes-Administration/Short-Term-Rentals/Applying-for-a-Permit.aspx.

62. Metro Gov't of Nashville & Davidson Cty., Tenn., Nashville Codes Administration, *Short Term Rental Property Operation Rules and Requirements*, https://www.nashville.gov/Codes-Administration/Short-Term-Rentals/Operation-Requirements.aspx.

63. SAVANNAH, GA., CODE OF ORDINANCES § 8-3025 ("Regulation as to uses"), https://library.municode.com/ga/savannah/codes/code_of_ordinances?nodeId=DIVIICOGEOR_PT8PLREDE_CH3ZO_ARTBZODI_S8-3025REUS.

64. *Id.* § 8-11013.

65. *Id.* § 8-3025.

66. COLUMBUS BUS. REGULATION § LICENSING CODE ch. 598.

The Columbus ordinance is unique in that it expressly addresses—and regulates—STR platforms (see *supra* section I).[67] It also requires hosts to retain all STR rental records for at least four years and to document the name of each STR guest responsible for making a reservation, the dates and duration of the stay, and the nightly rate charged for each reservation.[68] Also unique to the Columbus provision is the fact that it informs hosts that they will be denied a permit, or the renewal thereof, if the rental property has evidenced a pattern of felony drug-related activity, prostitution, human trafficking, or gang-related activity.[69] Unlike some cities that have regulated with the primary goal of preserving affordable housing, Columbus, through its ordinance, seems to focus more on safety and creating a level regulatory playing field for all accommodation providers.

B. State Preemption

In this legal context, the term "preemption" is used to describe the principle that state law may supersede any inconsistent local regulation.[70] A few states have preempted the local regulation of STRs in some form or fashion. Arizona, Idaho, and Wisconsin, for example, have become "STR-friendly" states—each has passed laws that limit local authority to restrict the operation of STRs. In Arizona a municipality cannot limit the number of STR properties a host operates nor ban STRs from specific zoning districts.[71] Some municipal regulation is allowed, provided the city demonstrates that it is aimed at safeguarding the public health and welfare.[72] This means that a local government in Arizona may require STR hosts to register their properties and abide by certain safety or operational requirements, but it cannot cap or ban STR ownership. The same holds true in Idaho.[73] In Wisconsin,

---

67. *Id.* § 598.04.

68. *Id.* § 598.04(C). Local governments in North Carolina should be mindful that regulations of this sort may pose privacy concerns. It is probably reasonable to require a host to track the number of nights rented and the nightly rate charged for tax purposes, but requiring the host to log personal information pertaining to each guest may violate the Fourth Amendment to the U.S. Constitution.

69. *Id.* § 598.05.

70. *See preemption*, BLACK'S LAW DICTIONARY (10th ed. 2014) (defining "preemption" in terms of federal law preempting inconsistent state law or regulation).

71. ARIZ. REV. STAT. § 9-500.39.

72. ARIZ. REV. STAT. § 9-500.39B.1.

73. IDAHO CODE § 67-6539 (prohibiting cities and counties from enacting "any ordinance that has the express or practical effect of prohibiting short-term rentals or vacation rentals. A county or city may implement such reasonable regulations as it deems necessary to safeguard the public health, safety and general welfare in order to protect the integrity of residential neighborhoods[.]").

municipalities and counties are prohibited from banning the rental of a residential dwelling for seven days or longer.[74] This means that week-long rentals are permitted regardless of zoning classification, but state law does not prevent local governments from prohibiting nightly rentals lasting fewer than seven consecutive days in certain zoning districts.

New York, by contrast, is trying to rein in short-term rentals. The state's Multiple Dwelling Law is particularly restrictive when it comes to these properties, prohibiting the short-term rental of "class A" multiple dwelling property for a duration of fewer than thirty days.[75] A *class A multiple dwelling* is defined as a multiple dwelling (e.g., apartment, duplex, studio apartment) that is occupied for permanent residence purposes.[76] This means that all the apartments advertised in New York City on Airbnb are technically illegal. The state has even passed a law banning the advertisement of STRs located within multiple dwelling buildings.[77] Violators are subject to a civil penalty of not more than $1,000 for a first violation, $5,000 for a second violation, and $7,500 for the third and subsequent violations.[78]

Further, New York City passed a law in 2018 to require Airbnb to disclose its hosts' personal information.[79] Airbnb challenged the law. In *Airbnb, Inc. v. City of New York*, a federal district court judge struck down the law on the basis that it is a potential violation of the Fourth Amendment to the U.S. Constitution to require the home-sharing platform to disclose user records.[80] The court held that there was no merit in the City's argument that home-sharing platforms do not have a protected privacy interest in the data sought because the data relates to the users of the platforms and not to the platforms themselves.[81]

Massachusetts has taken aggressive measures to level the playing field between hotels and short-term rental owners, particularly when it comes to taxation. A law passed in December 2018, to take effect July 1, 2019, mandates that all STR hosts register with the commonwealth and carry $1 million in liability insurance

---

74. Wis. Stat. Ann. § 66.1014.
75. N.Y. Mult. Dwell. Law § 4.8.
76. *Id.*
77. *Id.* § 121.
78. *Id.* at § 121.2.
79. N.Y. City Admin. Code § 26-2101-5 (referred to as "Local Law 146").

Airbnb listings do not include a host's full name, e-mail address, or telephone number, nor do they feature the rental property's exact address. Airbnb allows hosts and guests to privately communicate with each other over the platform. If an agreement is reached, Airbnb will disclose the listing address to the guest.

80. Nos. 18 Civ. 7712, 7742 (PAE), 2019 WL 91990, at *10 (S.D.N.Y. Jan. 3, 2019) ("This line of authority makes clear that the compelled production from home-sharing platforms of user records is an event that implicates the Fourth Amendment.").
81. *Id.*

coverage.[82] The law also expands the state's hotel and motel tax to include short-term rentals, meaning STR hosts must pay the 5.7 percent hotel tax that had previously only been levied on other types of accommodation providers. That's not all—municipalities may assess their own hotel tax of up to 6 percent (6.5 percent in Boston) under the new provision, and a community impact fee of up to 3 percent may be assessed locally on professionally managed properties (i.e., hosts who own more than two STRs in one jurisdiction).[83]

C. North Carolina Regulations

1. City of Asheville

To help curb a growing affordable housing problem, Asheville became one of the first cities in North Carolina to adopt STR regulations. The city defines *homestay STRs* and *whole-house STRs* (see *supra* section I) as separate uses and has relied on its zoning authority to restrict whole-house STRs from nearly all zoning districts. Presently, STRs may operate in Asheville's Resort District and are permitted by right in the Central Business Expansion, Lodging Expansion, and Mixed-Use Expansion districts.[84] The city will allow hosts to operate homestays in residential zones, provided the host meets certain criteria, including paying the $208 application and technology fee, providing proof of residency, and submitting an owner's affidavit evidencing the owner's authority or permission to apply for the homestay zoning permit.[85]

2. City of Brevard

While Brevard does not require STR hosts to apply for zoning permits, it has taken steps to define short-term rentals as a separate lodging use.[86] Under its Unified Development Ordinance, the city classifies STRs as property rentals of less than thirty days' duration and has capped the overnight occupancy at no more than two

---

82. 2018 Mass. Acts ch. 337, "An Act Regulating and Insuring Short-Term Rentals," § 9 (adding a new section, 4F, to Mass. Gen. Laws ch. 175), https://malegislature.gov/Laws/SessionLaws/Acts/2018/Chapter337.

83. *Id.* § 6 (striking out and replacing sections 1 through 6 of Mass. Gen. Laws ch. 64G).

84. Asheville, N.C., Code § 7-8-1, https://library.municode.com/nc/asheville/codes/code_of_ordinances?nodeId=PTIICOOR_CH7DE_ARTVIIIGEUSEXDI_S7-8-1ENDEDIDEDIOFZOMA.

85. City of Asheville, N.C., Dev. Servs. Dep't, Homestay Permit Application, https://form.jotform.us/80596045369163.

86. City of Brevard, N.C., Code of Ordinances, Unified Dev. Ordinance § 3.34, https://library.municode.com/nc/brevard/codes/code_of_ordinances?nodeId=UNDEOR_CH3ADUSST_3.34SHRMRE.

Figure 2. Six North Carolina Cities and Towns That Regulate Short-Term Rentals*

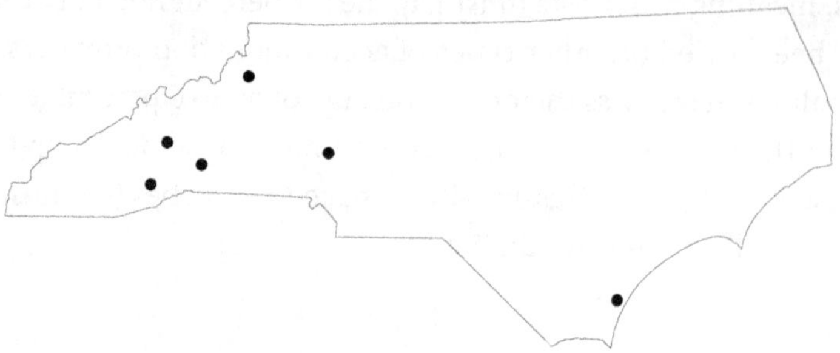

**Note*: This map is not meant to depict a complete picture of cities and towns with STR regulations in place. There may be other municipalities that regulate STRs.

persons per bedroom plus two additional persons.[87] Hosts are required to follow parking requirements that are based on the type of dwelling unit being rented. This includes two spaces for a primary residence and one space for any accessory unit.[88]

3. City of Wilmington

In June 2018, the Wilmington City Council adopted an ordinance to approve whole-house STRs in certain commercial and mixed-use districts and to approve homestay lodging in all residential, commercial, and mixed-use zoning districts.[89] A "homestay lodging" is defined under the ordinance as a "business engaged in the rental of individual bedrooms within a dwelling unit that serves as a host's principal residence, including any single-family or accessory apartment, that provides lodging for pay, for a maximum continuous period of twenty-nine (29) days, that does not include serving food, and to which the definition of family does not apply."[90] A "homestay host" is "a permanent, full-time resident of a property who is present during the homestay term for the entire time lodgers are staying on the property."[91] In February 2019, the city council voted to expand the areas in which whole-house STRs are allowed to operate to include certain residential zoning districts.[92]

---

87. *Id.* §§ A., B.1., respectively.

88. *Id.* § B.3 (referencing Chapter 10 of the Unified Development Ordinance).

89. *See* WILMINGTON, N.C., CODE OF ORDINANCES, LAND DEV. CODE, §§ 18-177 through -182, -184 through -185, -187 through -191, -193 through -196, -200, -202, -204, -267, -277, -289, -305, -329 through -330, -532, -812, -852, https://library.municode.com/nc/wilmington/codes/code_of_ordinances?nodeId=PTIIITECO_CH18LADECO_ART5ZODIRE_DIVIIDIRE_S18-177R-REDI.

90. *Id.* § 18-812.

91. *Id.*

92. *See id.* §§ 18-177 through -182, -184, -187 through -189, -331. *See also* City of Wilmington, N.C., *Short-Term Lodging*, "Where Can [Homestays and Whole-House Lodgings] Be Located?", https://www.wilmingtonnc.gov/departments/planning-development-and-transportation/short-term-lodging.

Hosts of both whole-house STRs and homestays are required to obtain zoning permits and to comply with specified operational standards. This includes a requirement to maintain a commercial general liability insurance policy with a total limit of not less than $500,000 per each occurrence of bodily injury and property damage and to comply with local building and fire codes.[93] The ordinance prohibits "parties, events, classes, weddings, receptions, and large gatherings" in STRs.[94]

4. Town of Blowing Rock

Blowing Rock has adopted an STR ordinance[95] and plans to start enforcement of it in spring 2019.[96] The ordinance limits STRs to certain zoning districts and requires property owners with residences in those zones to apply for a zoning permit for each dwelling unit that is to be rented for fewer than twenty-eight consecutive days.[97] The permit must be renewed annually and is not valid until a safety inspection is completed. Among other requirements, the town requires sufficient off-street parking; operable smoke and carbon monoxide detectors; a local contact person (or management company) who is available to respond to complaints within two hours; and the posting on the front of the dwelling unit, in 3.5-inch reflective numbers, the 911 address.[98]

5. Town of Cornelius

STR hosts in Cornelius may receive a "Transient Occupancy Permit" for each residence used for transient occupancy (i.e., STR).[99] The town, however, has limited transient rentals to one individual tenancy within a seven-consecutive-calendar-day period, whether the residence is occupied or not.[100] This means that STR properties may only have one transient occupancy per week. Regarding STRs, the town bans exterior signage, requires a local contact person to be available twenty-four hours a day to address complaints relating the property, and prohibits special events to

---

93. *Id.* §§ 18-330(7), (6), respectively.

94. *Id.* § 18-330(10)e. (written notice of this ban on activities must be "conspicuously posted" in STR units).

95. Blowing Rock, N.C., Town Code, Land Use Ordinance § 16-10.12. The authors have a draft of adopted regulations for Blowing Rock on file.

96. E-mail from Kevin Rothrock, Planning Director, Town of Blowing Rock, to authors (Feb. 5, 2019) (on file with authors) (indicating enforcement start date of March 2019).

97. Blowing Rock, N.C., Town Code, Land Use Ordinance § 16-10.12.1 (STRs allowed in the following districts: CB, TC, GB, OI, Chetola Resort, and Royal Oaks Condominiums (overlay district). Certain properties in other zoning districts have been grandfathered in. Check ordinance for details.).

98. *Id.* § 16-10.12.(f) (on file with authors).

99. Town of Cornelius, N.C., Land Dev. Code § 6.2.45, https://www.cornelius.org/DocumentCenter/View/1616/CH-06-Uses-Permitted-With-Conditions?bidId=.

100. *Id.* § 6.2.45B.

North Carolina Cities, by the Numbers

North Carolina residents who rented out their homes on Airbnb in 2017 made a collective $97 million.* Top earners, by city, include the following:

- *Asheville*: $19.8 million
- *Charlotte*: $8.7 million
- *Wilmington*: $3.9 million
- *Raleigh*: $3.8 million
- *Durham*: $3.1 million
- *Boone*: $2.3 million
- *Kill Devil Hills*: $2.2 million
- *Black Mountain*: $1.4 million

*Camila Molina, *NC Residents Are Making Extra Cash on Airbnb. Here's How Much and Where*, News & Observer (Raleigh) (Jan. 23, 2018), https://www.newsobserver.com/news/local/article196151729.html.

be held on-site.[101] There is an occupancy cap of three persons per bedroom and a vehicle cap of two cars on-site per bedroom.[102]

6. Town of Lake Lure

Lake Lure allows residential vacation rentals (STRs) in most zoning districts. The town defines the term "residential vacation rental" as the rental of any part of a single-family dwelling or duplex for occupancy for a period of fewer than thirty days.[103] Homeowners must apply for a "Vacation Rental Operating Permit" and comply with the operational standards adopted by the town.[104] These operational regulations include occupancy caps, parking and trash provisions, and the requirement that the 24/7 contact information for the rental be posted on the exterior of the dwelling unit.[105] The town also requires an initial safety inspection prior to issuing a zoning permit and asks each host to provide an inspection report from a qualified plumber of the STR property's sewer system integrity and a leak-free connection to the town sewer.[106] A listing of these standards, as well as the application process, can be found on the town's website.[107]

101. *Id.* §§ 6.2.45E., I., R., respectively.

102. *Id.* §§ 6.2.45H., F., respectively.

103. *See* Town of Lake Lure, N.C., Residential Vacation Rentals, "What Are Residential Vacation Rentals?", TownofLakeLure.com, http://www.townoflakelure.com/residential-vacation-rentals.php.

104. Lake Lure, N.C., Town Ordinances, Zoning Regulations § 92.042(A)(2), https://www.egovlink.com/public_documents300/lakelure/published_documents/Town%20Ordinances/Chapter_92_Zoning_Regulations.pdf.

105. *See id.* § 92.042(A)(5).

106. *See id.* §§ 92.042(A)(4), (3), respectively; *see also* Town of Lake Lure, Certificate of Zoning Compliance, https://www.egovlink.com/public_documents300/lakelure/published_documents/Forms_Permits_Applications/Land%20Use/Vacation%20Rental%20Operating%20Permit%20Application.pdf (includes Vacation Rental Operating Permit checklist).

107. *See supra* note 104.

IV. Clarifying Short-Term Rental Regulatory Goals

As the above section evidences, municipal regulation of short-term rentals (STRs) can take many forms. A local government may want to take a phased approach when deciding which regulations will best serve its citizens. Specifically, there are four key phases that, if followed, will help produce an effective STR ordinance. By devoting attention to each of these phases, a local government will increase the likelihood that any proposed regulations will be both responsive to the community's needs and enforceable.

The Four Phases of Ordinance Adoption

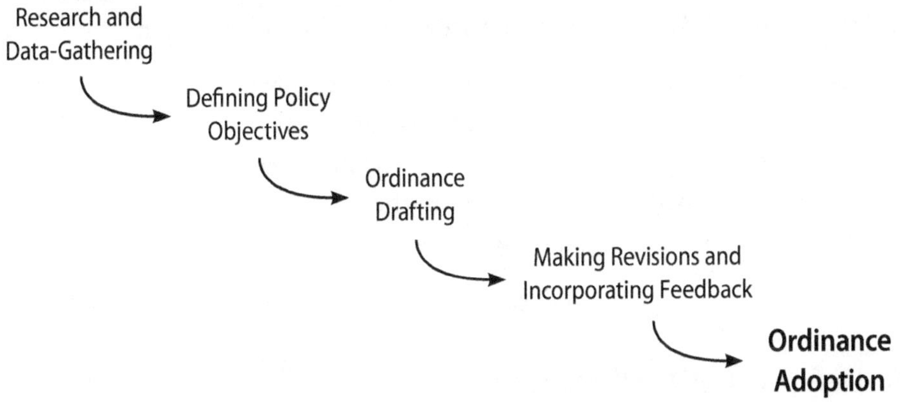

A. Research and Data-Gathering

Before sitting down to draft an STR ordinance, it is recommended that a local government first engage in a research and data-gathering phase to better understand the local STR market. In fact, many local governments in North Carolina have expressed an interest in better understanding or quantifying the effects Airbnb is having in their jurisdictions. During the research and data-gathering phase, a local government should compile both quantitative and qualitative data related to the tourist economy. It should also identify community needs in this area.

1. Quantitative Data

It is helpful to gather quantitative data about STR listings to get a sense of the local STR market. Below are a few questions local governments might consider when conducting this research; many of the answers may be available through AirDNA, Airbnb's data and analytics platform.[108] For a small fee, AirDNA turns vacation

108. AirDNA, https://www.airdna.co/.

rental data from Airbnb and HomeAway into actionable analytics for given locations. Suggested questions for local governments include the following:

- How many listings are there in our community?
- Where are current listings located and are there areas of concentration?
- What type, size, and occupancy levels of housing are offered?
- What is the average listing price and what is the range of prices for listings?
- Do existing lodging options meet transient accommodations needs?[109]

2. Qualitative Data

Understanding the context of STRs within a local community is also advisable for community leaders. A local government may want to host public comment forums to learn about permanent residents' positions and opinions surrounding STR regulations.[110] Consider the following context-driven questions:

- What is the general attitude in the community toward STRs?
- Who, exactly, is concerned about the issue?
- How are complaints about STRs currently handled?
- Are STRs defined as a separate use in the local zoning ordinance?
- Are there gaps or ambiguities in the existing law?

B. Defining Policy Objectives

Following the research and data-gathering phase, local governments should work to define the specific policy objective(s) that would be promoted by new STR regulations.[111] Simply put, the policy objectives are the stated goals of any new regulations.[112] These policy objectives should stem directly from the needs identified in the research and data-gathering phase of the ordinance-adoption process. Below are some of the more common policy arguments advanced by local governments in support of STR regulation.

---

109. Rachel Keyser, *A Guide to Smart AirBnB Regulation for Local Governments*, VIEWPOINT (Oct. 24, 2016), http://www.viewpointcloud.com/blog/local-government-resources/airbnb-regulation-guide/ (outlining some common questions raised when gathering quantitative and qualitative data for STR regulation).

110. *Id.* ("Public comment forums will help get a pulse on residents' opinions.")

111. Ulrik Binzer, *Whitepaper: A Practical Guide to Effectively Regulating Short-Term Rentals on the Local Government Level*, HOSTCOMPLIANCE.COM (2016), https://hostcompliance.com/resources-gallery/a-practical-guide-to-effectively-regulating-short-term-rentals-on-the-local-government-level.

112. *Id.*

Quiz: Data Gathering

Facts: Town officials are being pressured by a small group of citizens to ban the short-term rental of lake-front properties that are commonly rented to tourists in summer months. These citizens argue that the lake has become overcrowded with large groups of transient renters who are disturbing the peace and welfare of the community. What is the first step town officials should take before deciding whether to move forward with regulations?

Answer: Town officials should first seek to gather quantitative and qualitative data regarding the local STR market. This includes knowing where these properties operate and the average overnight occupancy per rental. Town officials may also want to consider how a ban on STRs within a certain zoning district would affect the local economy.

1. Regulating STRs Maximizes Housing Availability and Affordability

Historically, when STRs have been restricted by local governments to certain non-residential zoning districts, it has often been to further the goal of maximizing the availability of affordable housing within residential areas. Both nationally and globally, local officials are concerned that the explosive growth of STRs has led to a crippling housing shortage for permanent residents due to increased rents and fewer units available for long-term habitation. By restricting the number of STRs allowed to operate within a designated geographic area, local officials hope that additional housing stock will become available. In North Carolina, the preservation of affordable housing will likely be a top policy objective for densely populated municipalities that are also attractive tourist destinations.

2. Regulating STRs Preserves Neighborhood Character

One policy objective with strong legal backing by the U.S. Supreme Court is the need to preserve the character of neighborhoods in communities large and small.[113] Homeowners nationwide have voiced concerns that STRs "take the 'neighbor' out of neighborhoods."[114] Some have argued that when a neighborhood becomes occupied

---

113. Vill. of Euclid v. Ambler Realty Co., 272 U.S. 365, 395 (1926) (holding that the preservation of neighborhood character constitutes a valid exercise of a jurisdiction's police power); Vill. of Belle Terre v. Boraas, 416 U.S. 1, 9 (1974) ("The police power is not confined to elimination of filth, stench, and unhealthy places. It is ample to lay out zones where family values, youth values, and the blessings of quiet seclusion and clean air make the area a sanctuary for people.").

114. David J. Brown, *Do Short-Term Vacation Rentals Change the Character of Historic Neighborhoods?*, Preservation Leadership Forum (July 27, 2017), https://forum.savingplaces.org/blogs/david-brown/2017/07/25/do-short-term-vacation-rentals-change-the-character-of-historic-neighborhoods.

by transients who do not vote, attend school, or otherwise have any vested interest in its upkeep, the charm and character of the place, as well as the appeal of living there, starts to dwindle.[115] When it comes to developing and implementing specific policies related to the preservation of neighborhood character, local governments have a variety of options available to them, including restricting "party houses" to cut down on neighborhood noise and safety levels or taking more general action to minimize the parking problems sometimes associated with STRs.[116] Each of these options, if achieved, would help preserve neighborhood character.

3. Regulating STRs Provides for the Health and Safety of Others

Nearly all jurisdictions that seek to regulate STRs adopt the planning objective of ensuring that guests and community residents alike remain healthy and safe.

4. Regulating STRs Generates Occupancy Tax Revenue

Another common policy objective of STR regulation is to ensure that STR hosts pay their share of local taxes, including the occupancy tax and personal property taxes.[117] The collection of occupancy taxes is discussed in greater detail in section VIII, *infra*.

5. Regulating STRs Provides Regulatory Consistency

A concern frequently voiced by hotel, motel, and B&B owners is that the regulatory playing field is uneven between them and STR hosts. This is generally true—these accommodation providers must comply with local health, safety, and inspection requirements that may not be required of STRs. While the regulations applicable to STRs need not be identical to those covering the other types of lodgings, introducing some type of regulatory oversight of STRs will likely help bolster goodwill between local governments and the more traditional transient accommodation providers.

C. Ordinance Drafting

When the first two phases of the ordinance-adoption process—research and data-gathering and defining policy objectives—are complete, a local government can begin to draft STR regulations. Local governments are advised to consider their actual enforcement capabilities during the ordinance-drafting process.

---

115. *Id.*

116. *Id.*

117. It is worth noting that Airbnb now remits occupancy taxes directly to local tax offices. This fact does not diminish the value or relevance of this policy objective, however, as other local taxes are involved in STR regulation.

If a local government lacks the means to enforce new STR regulations, hosts will be less likely to comply with regulatory requirements.

1. Defining "Short-Term Rental"

The crucial first step in the ordinance-drafting phase of STR regulation by local governments is for the regulators to decide on a definition of *short-term rental.* Regardless of what definition emerges, a short-term rental should be a distinguishable land use in the jurisdiction's land development code. Other STR-related terms should also be clearly defined. For example, if a local government has decided to regulate homestays (home-sharing rentals), it should also define that particular land use.

Below are examples of how a few North Carolina cities have defined STRs and homestays.

Asheville

> *"Homestay means a private, resident occupied dwelling unit, with up to two guest rooms where overnight lodging accommodations are provided to transients for compensation and where the use is subordinate and incidental to the main residential use of the building. A homestay is considered a 'lodging' use under this [Unified Development Ordinance or] UDO."*[118]
>
> *"Short-term vacation rental means a dwelling unit with up to six guest rooms that is used and/or advertised through an online platform, or other media, for transient occupancy for a period of less than one month. A short-term vacation rental is considered a 'Lodging' use under this UDO."*[119]

Blowing Rock

> *"Short-Term Rental of a Dwelling Unit. The rental, lease, or use of an attached or detached residential dwelling unit for a duration that is less than 28 consecutive days. Short-term rental does not include rooming houses, boarding houses, or bed and breakfast establishments, which are specifically addressed as separate uses within the Table of Permissible Uses."*[120]

Wilmington

> *"Homestay lodging—The business engaged in the rental of individual bedrooms within a dwelling unit that serves as a host's principal residence, including any single-family or accessory apartment, that provides lodging*

---

118. Asheville, N.C., Code § 7-2-5, https://library.municode.com/nc/asheville/codes/code_of_ordinances?nodeId=PTIICOOR_CH7DE_ARTIIOFMARUCODE_S7-2-5DE.

119. *Id.*

120. Blowing Rock, N.C., Town Code, Land Use Ordinance § 16-2.2, http://www.townofblowingrocknc.gov/home/showdocument?id=244.

for pay, for a maximum continuous period of twenty-nine (29) days, that does not include serving food, and which the definition of family does not apply."[121]

"Whole-house lodging: A business engaged in the rental of an entire dwelling unit that provides lodging for pay, for a maximum continuous period of twenty-nine (29) days and does not include the serving of food. Whole-house lodging uses are exempt from the definition of 'family.'"[122]

2. Understanding Regulatory Options

Once a local government has defined "short-term rental," it must then decide what types of regulations it wants to adopt related to such properties. There are three main categories of STR regulations: (1) geographical restrictions, (2) quantitative restrictions, and (3) operational requirements.[123] It is worth noting that these regulations are not either/or. Most zoning regulations include a combination of geographic, quantitative, and operational limits. As mentioned above, jurisdictions may approach STR regulation differently, and thus it is important for a local government to consider its enforcement capabilities when deciding what types of regulations to impose.

a. Geographic Regulations

A local government may rely on its zoning authority to regulate STRs based on their zoning classification (i.e., their location). This is a powerful tool that can prove particularly helpful for communities dealing with affordable housing issues. A local government may first want to tackle the question of whether it should allow STRs in residentially-zoned districts. This is a simple—but often controversial—question. Local officials in Raleigh have been grappling with it for some time now, with residents holding strong opinions on both sides of the issue. In areas that are heavily dependent on tourism and in which current accommodation providers cannot meet tourist demands, it will probably be beneficial to allow hosts to operate STRs in all zoning districts.

A local government also must determine in which commercial, mixed-use, or other zones it will allow STRs. Remember, as stated above, that in some juris-

---

121. WILMINGTON, N.C., CODE OF ORDINANCES, LAND DEV. CODE § 18-812, https://library.municode.com/nc/wilmington/codes/code_of_ordinances?nodeId=PTIIITECO_CH18LADECO_ART15DE_S18-812DE.

122. *Id.*

123. Jamila Jefferson-Jones, *Can Short-Term Rental Arrangements Increase Home Values? A Case for AirBNB and other Home Sharing Arrangements*, CORNELL REAL EST. REV. 13(1), 12–19 (2015), https://scholarship.sha.cornell.edu/cgi/viewcontent.cgi?article=1133&context=crer (discussing five common categories of STR regulations).

dictions it may be unlawful to ban STRs in all zoning districts except in special circumstances. This is because of a presumption that a jurisdiction should find a place within its boundaries for all lawful land uses.[124] Asheville has relied on its zoning authority to limit the operation of STRs in most of its zoning districts. While some STRs have been grandfathered into other zoning districts, the city presently only allows new STRs in the Resort District, but STRs are permitted by right in the Central Business Expansion, Lodging Expansion, and Mixed-Use Expansion districts.[125] Thus, Asheville has taken measures to heavily restrict the areas in which STRs may lawfully operate.

b. Quantitative Regulations

i. Capping the Number of Permits Issued

A local government, for example, a city, may decide to place a cap on the number of STR permits it will issue. In doing so, it may either cap the total number of permits issued citywide or cap the number of permits issued for different zoning districts. One benefit of instituting a cap is that the local government can allow STRs to lawfully operate in all districts, while at the same time limiting their growth and regulating population density. Capping the number of permits issued may be viewed by some as a compromise. Savannah, Ga., has implemented a 20-percent-per-ward cap on the permits it issues to "not-owner-occupied" STRs within its historic and conservation districts.[126] Santa Fe, N.M., simply caps the total number of STR permits it issues.[127]

ii. Capping the Number of Units That May Be Used as STRs

Investors sometimes purchase multiple units within a multi-unit building for the sole purpose of renting the units on a short-term basis. Developers of new construction are now earmarking certain units, floors, or even entire buildings for use as short-term rentals.[128] These developers market the properties to investors

124. *See supra* section II.A for more on this topic.

125. ASHEVILLE, N.C., CODE § 7-8-1, https://library.municode.com/nc/asheville/codes/code_of_ordinances?nodeId=PTIICOOR_CH7DE_ARTVIIIGEUSEXDI_S7-8-1ENDEDIDEDIOFZOMA.

126. *See* City of Savannah, *Short-Term Vacation Rental Update*, "Per-Ward Cap," https://www.savannahga.gov/2327/STVR-Regulation-Updates.

127. *See* SANTA FE, N.M., CODE OF ORDINANCES, LAND DEV. CODE § 14-6.2(A)(5)(b)(iii), https://library.municode.com/nm/santa_fe/codes/code_of_ordinances?nodeId=CH14LADE_ART14-6PEUSUSRE_14-6.2UECST ("The land use director may issue rental permits in a quantity approved by the governing body through adoption, after a public hearing, of a resolution for residential units not otherwise qualifying for permits . . .").

128. For example, YOTLEPAD Miami is a thirty-floor condominium building currently under construction in downtown Miami, Fla., that is completely exempt from

as prime short-term rental opportunities. This has left some local governments scrambling to enact regulations that stop multi-unit dwellings from turning into de facto hotels. Austin, Tex., has addressed this concern by mandating that that no more that 25 percent of units within a multi-unit building in a commercial district be granted a Type 3 vacation rental license (applicable to not-owner-occupied multifamily-use properties).[129]

iii. Capping the Number of Nights That a Property May Be Used as an STR

Another regulatory option for local governments is to limit the total number of nights that a property may be rented each year. For example, San Francisco only allows hosts to conduct "un-hosted" STRs for a maximum of ninety days per year. Once the ninety-day limit is reached, hosts are restricted to homestay rentals in which they must be present for the duration of the rental period.[130] This type of regulation effectively limits STR hosts to renting their primary residences and dissuades investors from purchasing multiple properties exclusively for STR use.

c. *Operational Regulations*

Operational regulations incorporate performance-like standards to address issues such as unit characteristics, host operation, and guest requirements. Below is a discussion of some of the more common STR operational regulations. Not every jurisdiction will have a need for each of the operational regulations listed below, and it is important to consider enforcement capabilities when deciding which of these types of regulations to adopt.

i. Occupancy Limits

Placing restrictions on the number of occupants allowed to stay overnight at a given property is one way to help minimize noise complaints and cut down on the use of STR units as "party houses." Most jurisdictions that regulate STRs have included an occupancy provision within their STR ordinances. They have done so for a variety of reasons, including to protect the safety of the occupants and to

---

STR regulations. Buyers are given a guarantee that they will be able to rent their condo units on a short-term basis without having to register them or otherwise comply with local STR regulations. Aly J. Yale, *10 Years After Airbnb, Real Estate Developers See the Money in Home-Sharing*, FORBES (Oct. 17, 2018), https://www.forbes.com/sites/alyyale/2018/10/17/multi-family-developers-are-leveraging-the-short-term-rental-fad-heres-how/#154dd5e638e0.

129. AUSTIN, TEX., LAND DEV. CODE § 25-2-791(C)(5), https://library.municode.com/tx/austin/codes/land_development_code?nodeId=TIT25LADE_CH25-2ZO_SUBCHAPTER_CUSDERE_ART4ADRECEUS_SPCRESHRMREUS_S25-2-791LIRE.

130. San Francisco Office of Short-Term Rentals, *Become a Certified Host*, SHORTTERMRENTALS.SF.GOV, https://shorttermrentals.sfgov.org/hosting/become-certified ("Rent a portion or your entire unit for less than 30 consecutive nights while you are not present (un-hosted rentals), for a maximum of 90 nights per calendar year.").

Quiz: Occupancy Caps

Facts: A resort town in North Carolina has decided to allow short-term rentals (STRs) in every zoning district, subject to a variety of operational regulations. The local government wants, in its ordinance, to cap the occupancy of STRs at a maximum of twelve persons. Local officials are aware that a few of the homes in the community can accommodate much larger overnight occupancies and are often used as special events spaces for weddings, receptions, and parties. The local government wants to allow these larger-scale properties to continue to operate, but, were it to do so, the maximum occupancy limit set forth in the ordinance would be violated. Can the local government separately regulate certain properties that are suitable for use as special event spaces?

Answer: Yes. For large properties that can accommodate many overnight guests or for properties that make suitable special-event spaces, the local government can require property owners to apply for a special- or conditional-use permit. The decision on whether to grant these permits is quasi-judicial in nature, and it is within the discretion of the community's governing board or board of adjustment to grant or deny permit requests. Owners of these large properties would be exempt from any ordinance requirement to apply for an STR permit because the property use would be different from than that of an STR.

control population density in an area. Whether and how to regulate occupancy are questions that should be considered by all local governments.

A typical occupancy regulation limits the number of occupants based on the number bedrooms in a property. For example, Nashville, Tenn., has a maximum occupancy provision in its ordinance that limits the number of occupants in an STR at any one time to no more than twice the number of sleeping rooms in the unit plus four.[131] The Nashville ordinance also requires that the occupancy limit to be "conspicuously" posted within the rental unit and provides that advertising for more occupants than allowed by the regulation shall be grounds for revocation of the STR permit.[132]

In North Carolina, builders in coastal areas have constructed large homes that include twelve or more bedrooms. While these properties are attractive to tourists hosting events or traveling with a large group of friends or family, the fact that these properties are occupied by twenty or more persons at one time may be a concern for local officials. Communities that seek to limit the total number of overnight occupants in a residence may want to adopt an ordinance provision

---

131. Code of Metro. Gov't of Nashville & Davidson Cty., Tenn., § 17.16.070U.4.f., https://library.municode.com/tn/metro_government_of_nashville_and_davidson_county/codes/code_of_ordinances?nodeId=CD_TIT17ZO_CH17.16LAUSDEST_ARTIIUSPECOPC_17.16.070COUS.

132. *Id.*

mandating that short-term rental properties be occupied by no more than X number of persons, regardless of the number of bedrooms. For example:

> The overnight occupancy of an STR shall not exceed two (2) persons per bedroom plus two (2) additional persons. The maximum number of guests in a short-term rental is limited to fifteen (15) persons, excluding children under three (3) years of age.

Based on this provision, a residence with twenty bedrooms would still have an occupancy cap of fifteen persons. In areas where properties are on a septic system, the system capacity is sometimes used as the basis for calculating the occupancy cap.

ii. Parking Restrictions

In downtown areas, beach towns, and other tourist spots, parking can be a major issue for local governments. This issue is exacerbated by the fact that homes that were not previously rented out before the home-sharing boom are now occupied by renters. To address the matter a local government may rely on the parking regulations already set forth in its zoning unified development ordinance (UDO) and set new guidelines when it comes to STRs. For example, the Nashville STR ordinance (1) states that "Parking shall be provided as required by Section 17.20.030" of the city's Metropolitan Code and (2) clarifies that STR guests are prohibited from parking recreational vehicles, buses, or trailers on the street or on the STR property.[133] One Utah county mandates that a minimum of one parking spot per bedroom be allocated for STRs; it also prohibits guests from bringing more cars than the number of parking spots provided—i.e., it bans parking cars on the lawns of STR properties.[134] To ensure that parking is available for guests, it is not uncommon to ask hosts to submit a site plan with their application for an STR license.[135] In Wilmington, NC, STR guests must display a parking placard in some zoning districts.

---

133. *Id.* § 17.16.070U.4.c. (requiring that "[n]o recreational vehicles, buses, or trailers shall be visible on the street or property in conjunction with the STR[] use").

134. Daggett Cty., Utah, Cty. Code § 8-15-6.B., https://www.sterlingcodifiers.com/codebook/index.php?book_id=1058 ("Parking shall be provided, at a minimum, of one (1) vehicle per bedroom. . . . The number of vehicles allowed by the occupants of a short term rental home shall be restricted to the number of parking spaces provided by the owner.").

135. Tillamook Cty., Or., Ordinance No. 84, §9(B), https://www.co.tillamook.or.us/Documents/BOCCOrdinances/Ordinance%2084.pdf (short-term vacation rental permit application requires site plan showing required parking spots must be submitted with permit application).

iii. Noise Restrictions

Under many STR ordinances, STR guests are expected to follow "all applicable noise restrictions and regulations regarding the public peace and welfare," as provided for in the given jurisdiction's land use code or local ordinances.[136]

iv. Responsible Party Designation Requirement

Because STR hosts sometimes travel themselves while their properties are being rented, it is common to require them to designate a local responsible party who can be contacted in the event of an emergency. If the host or primary resident remains local during STR stays, he or she could be the designee.

Should a neighbor suspect that the community's maximum occupancy cap has been exceeded, he or she can call the designee to report the suspected ordinance violation.[137] A guest can contact the designee if he or she gets locked out of the STR unit or if there is a maintenance problem (e.g., a burst pipe). Whatever the concern, guests, neighbors, and local officials alike may feel an increased sense of security when there is a responsible party readily available to contact.

v. Requirement That Adjacent Property Owners Be Notified of STR Use

As part of the STR permit application process, a host may be required to provide written notice to neighboring property owners of the intended STR use of his or her property. However, such a mandate would likely be unnecessary in areas where houses are frequently rented on a short-term basis but there are few permanent residents. For example, if most houses on Emerald Isle, N.C., operate as year-round STRs, there is probably no need to require that hosts notify adjacent property owners of STR use—the neighbors are likely doing it too. In cases where this type of regulation would prove helpful, hosts may be asked to provide some or all the following information to adjacent owners:

- street address of the proposed STR,
- name of the property owner,
- location of on-site parking for STR occupants,
- contact information for the designated responsible party, and/or
- maximum occupancy requirements.[138]

---

136. *See, e.g.*, Code of Metro. Gov't of Nashville & Davidson Cty., Tenn., § 17.16.070U.4.a., https://library.municode.com/tn/metro_government_of_nashville_and_davidson_county/codes/code_of_ordinances?nodeId=CD_TIT17ZO_CH17.16LAUSDEST_ARTIIUSPECOPC_17.16.070COUS.

137. *Id.* § 17.16.070U.2.b.i. (requiting all STR permit applications to include "[t]he name, telephone number, address, and email address of the owner and of a person or business ('responsible party') residing or located within twenty-five miles of the STR[] that is responsible for addressing all maintenance and safety concerns").

138. *See* Savannah, Ga., Code of Ordinances § 11-8-10015, https://library.municode.com/ga/savannah/codes/code_of_ordinances?nodeId=DIVIICOGEOR_

It is up to each local government to determine what will constitute sufficient evidence that notice of intended STR use was given. Evidence of notification may include (1) a copy of the letter sent to neighbors and signed by each neighbor, along with each neighbor's full address and signature;[139] (2) a signed receipt of registered or certified U.S. mail addressed to property owners; or (3) notice from the U.S. Postal Service that registered or certified mail sent to an owner/owners was refused or not timely accepted.[140]

vi. Required Health and Safety Inspections

It is reasonable for local governments to require STRs to meet basic health and safety standards.[141] To do this, some jurisdictions require mandatory safety inspections before issuing an STR license. Both counties and cities in North Carolina have statutory authority to inspect properties.[142] Generally, such inspections are conducted by local government entities, including the fire department or the local planning department.[143] Mandating safety inspections has some drawbacks for local governments, including raising the administrative costs of the jurisdiction's STR regulatory program and possibly burdening local officials with increased inspection duties. There are other implementation issues to consider as well. Can the local government ensure that all active STRs are inspected in a timely manner? Will there be a grace period during which STRs may operate without an inspection until one can be conducted? Requiring hosts to cease all rental activity pending an inspection would likely be problematic, given that many properties are rented far into the future. It is important for each jurisdiction to consider its resources and decide on an implementation process before mandating property inspections.

In North Carolina, the Town of Lake Lure requires that a property undergo an initial inspection before it will issue a short-term vacation rental permit for the

---

PT8PLREDE_CH11SHRMVARE_S8-11015GRDEAP.

139. Tillamook Cty. Ordinance No. 84, § 9(D).

140. *See* Code of Metro. Gov't of Nashville & Davidson Cty. § 17.16.070U.2.b.iii., https://library.municode.com/tn/metro_government_of_nashville_and_davidson_county/codes/code_of_ordinances?nodeId=CD_TIT17ZO_CH17.16LAUSDEST_ARTIIUSPECOPC_17.16.070COUS (allowing for proof of notice to be made in one of the three ways noted in the text).

141. Eskandari-QuJar & Orsi, *supra* note 51, at 20 ("Cities should require STR hosts to adhere to basic standards for [the] health and safety of their guests.").

142. G.S 160A-411 (cities); 153A-351 (counties).

143. *See, e.g.*, Tillamook Cty. Ordinance No. 84, § 7(c) ("A permit shall not be issued until a short term rental passes inspection;" inspections are scheduled by the County Department of Community Development); Austin, Tex., Land Dev. Code § 25-2-791, https://library.municode.com/tx/austin/codes/land_development_code?nodeId=TIT25LADE_CH25-2ZO_SUBCHAPTER_CUSDERE_ART4ADRECEUS_SPCRESHRMREUS_S25-2-791LIRE (requiring permit applicants for vacation rentals (1) to submit their properties to, and to pass, "a minimum life-safety inspection" or (2) to have been issued a certificate of occupancy within ten years.).

Quiz: Health and Safety Inspections

Question: If a local government decides to regulate short-term rentals, is it required to inspect each property for compliance with local health and safety regulations?

Answer: No. The local government can mandate health and safety inspections, but it is not required to do so. A self-inspection checklist is one alternative to property inspections.

property, and a permit applicant must also provide an inspection report from a plumber evidencing a leak-free connection from the property to the town sewer.[144] Blowing Rock, N.C., also requires an on-site inspection before the town will issue an STR permit.[145] The City of Boulder, Colo., has devised a way to require property inspections for those seeking STR licenses without further burdening the local government. License applicants must hire a third-party inspection company to perform a basic safety inspection of their property, and a license will not be issued until the company certifies that the property is safe.[146] The city's website provides applicants with the names of several independent inspection providers but also directs applicants to the Yellow Pages® for additional resources.[147] For local governments that are set on mandating in-person inspections, Boulder's approach is one to consider. But keep in mind that local companies would need training and/or guidance on the necessary criteria for the safety inspections.

A less-involved model for a local government wishing to regulate health and safety issues surrounding STRs is to create a self-inspection checklist for hosts to complete and submit along with their license applications.[148] The self-inspection

144. Lake Lure, N.C., Town Ordinances, Zoning Regulations § 92.042(A)(4), https://www.egovlink.com/public_documents300/lakelure/published_documents/Town%20Ordinances/Chapter_92_Zoning_Regulations.pdf (requiring initial property inspection); *see also* Town of Lake Lure, Certificate of Zoning Compliance, https://www.egovlink.com/public_documents300/lakelure/published_documents/Forms_Permits_Applications/Land%20Use/Vacation%20Rental%20Operating%20Permit%20Application.pdf (includes Vacation Rental Operating Permit checklist, which requires certification from plumber of sewer system integrity).

145. Some STR regulations are set forth in Chapter 16 of the Blowing Rock Code, which is the town's Land Use Ordinance. The authors also have a draft of adopted regulations for Blowing Rock on file. As of this writing, the town has not yet begun to enforce its STR ordinance.

146. City of Boulder, Colo., *Rental Housing Licensing Inspections*, BoulderColorado.gov, https://bouldercolorado.gov/plan-develop/rental-housing-licensing-inspections.

147. *Id.*

148. Eskandari-QuJar & Orsi, *supra* note 51, at 20; *see also* Nederland, Colo., Mun. Code § 6-292(a), http://nederlandco.org/wp-content/uploads/2018/07/NED-ORD-short-term-rentals-after-6.18-PC-meeting.pdf (requiring a certification by the applicant that

checklist would align with local health and safety codes and may reference local code provisions directly. For example, a safety inspection checklist may ask the following question: "Is the premise equipped with operable smoke detectors within 15 feet of each sleeping area, as required by Section ___ of the Housing Code?" When the host-applicant signs the self-inspection checklist, this is tantamount to certifying, under penalty of perjury, compliance with the safety requirements set forth in the checklist.[149] For properties that were built within ten years of the permit application date, a local government should consider accepting a copy of the certificate of occupancy in lieu of a safety inspection checklist.

Below are a few safety-related questions that a jurisdiction may want to include in an STR self-inspection checklist.[150] Again, it is entirely up to each local government to determine whether and how it wants to regulate health and safety. Each local government will have differing needs and enforcement capabilities.

- Is the STR's address clearly posted on the exterior and interior of the property?
- Is there at least one working fire extinguisher in each STR unit that is easily accessible?
- Are all electrical outlets in the unit(s) covered by a faceplate?
- Do all exterior garbage cans and recycling bins have lids?
- Is there a working carbon monoxide detector located on each floor of the STR property?
- Is there a smoke detector within X feet of every sleeping area in the unit(s)?
- Does every sleeping area have an operable emergency escape (e.g., a window that opens)?

vii. Insurance Requirements

Although most STR stays are uneventful, it is important for hosts to have adequate insurance coverage in case of an unforeseen event. Because not all traditional homeowners' policies cover incidents that occur during an STR stay, Airbnb and

---

the STR unit is equipped with operational smoke detectors, carbon monoxide detectors, and fire extinguishers, as well as a completed STR self-inspection form, signed under penalty of perjury).

149. Along with submitting a self-inspection certification, at least one local government (a city) requires each STR host to sign a statement agreeing to indemnify, defend, and hold the city harmless from all claims and liabilities resulting from the STR. *See* Dana Point, Cal., Mun. Code § 5.38.050, https://qcode.us/codes/danapoint/?view=desktop&topic=5-5_38-5_38_050 (requiring "an executed agreement to indemnify, defend, and save the City harmless from any and all claims and liabilities of any kind whatsoever resulting from or arising out of the short-term rental").

150. *Authors' Note*: This is not a comprehensive list. Each jurisdiction should consult with the appropriate local officials when deciding what to include on any safety self-inspection checklist.

Table 1. Insurance Options from STR Platform Companies*

Platform	Liability Coverage	Real and Personal Property Damage Coverage
Airbnb[a]	Primary coverage up to $1 million	Coverage up to $1 million
HomeAway[b]	Coverage up to $1 million; to be filed with host's personal liability policy, and both policies will contribute to settling a claim	None
FlipKey/TripAdvisor Vacation Rentals[c]	None	None

*See each platform's terms and conditions for coverage details and exclusions.

a. Airbnb, Inc., *Host Protection Insurance*, Airbnb.com, https://www.airbnb.com/host-protection-insurance; Airbnb, Inc., *Host Guarantee Terms and Conditions*, Airbnb.com (last updated Feb. 20, 2019), https://www.airbnb.com/terms/host_guarantee (stating that "Airbnb agrees to pay you, as a Host, to repair or replace your Covered Property . . . damaged or destroyed as a result of a Covered Loss . . ., subject to the limitations, exclusions and conditions in the Host Guarantee Terms.").

b. HomeAway.com, Inc., *$1M Liability Insurance*, HomeAway.com https://www.homeaway.com/l/liability-insurance.

c. TripAdvisor Vacation Rentals, *What Do I Need to Know about Home/Property Insurance?*, TripAdvisor.com (2019), https://rentalsupport.tripadvisor.com/faq/view/What-do-I-need-to-know-about-home-property-insurance ("It's important to note that TripAdvisor Rentals doesn't provide any form of insurance to homeowners.").

HomeAway provide some type of liability coverage when rental transactions are conducted through their platforms. Local governments have also recognized the importance of ensuring that hosts have adequate coverage, and they sometimes require hosts to present evidence of commercial liability insurance coverage of a certain amount.[151] The Wilmington, N.C., STR ordinance requires that hosts carry a commercial general liability insurance policy with a total limit of not

151. *See, e.g.*, Code of Metro. Gov't of Nashville & Davidson Cty., Tenn., § 6.28.030.D.2. (enacted by Ordinance No. BL2014-951, Council of the Metro. Gov't of Nashville & Davidson Cty. (Feb. 26, 2016)), https://www.nashville.gov/mc/ordinances/term_2011_2015/bl2014_951.htm (requiring proof of fire, hazard, and liability (minimum of $1,000,000) coverage per occurrence); Savannah, Ga., Code of Ordinances § 11-8-10013(b)(4) (emphases added), https://library.municode.com/ga/savannah/codes/code_of_ordinances?nodeId=DIVIICOGEOR_PT8PLREDE_CH11SHRMVARE_S8-11013APSHRMVARECE (requiring "[p]roof of insurance **indicating the premises is used as a short-term vacation rental** . . ."); *see also* John Banczat, Katey Ferenzi, & Rachel Hartman, *Short Term Vacation Rental Liability Insurance Is Not Enough for Homeowners*, Turnkey Blog (May 24, 2017), https://blog.turnkeyvr.com/short-term-vacation-rental-liability-insurance/ ("[I]n most locations across the US you must show proof of $1M in liability insurance in order to receive a[] short term vacation rental permit.").

Table 2. Selected Local Regulations Covering Whole-House STRs*

Jurisdiction	STR Permit Required?	Occupancy Cap Required?	Insurance Required?	On-Site Inspection Required?	Necessary to Designated Responsible Party?	Specific Rules for Parking Spaces?
Asheville[a]	Yes	No, but STRs are defined as properties having no more than 6 guest rooms	Yes; no specified coverage amount	Yes	No	1 spot per 2 bedrooms (BRs) for lodging uses
Blowing Rock[b]	Yes	No	No	Yes	Yes	Property must have sufficient off-street parking
Brevard[c]	No	2 per BR, +2	No	No	No	2 spots for primary residence; 1 per accessory unit
Cornelius[d]	Yes	3 persons per BR	No	No	No	2 spots per BR
Lake Lure[e]	Yes	2, +4, max of 12	No	Yes	Yes	1 spot per 2 BRs
Wilmington[f]	Yes	No, but limited to 2% of parcels; 400 ft. separation between uses	Yes; $500,000 min.	Unknown	Yes	1 spot per BR

*Note that this list is not exhaustive. At the time of this writing, other jurisdictions were considering or may have adopted regulations.

a. Asheville, N.C., Code §§ 7-5-2, 7-16-1, 7-11-2.

b. Some STR regulations are set forth in Chapter 16 of the Blowing Rock Code, which is the town's Land Use Ordinance. The authors also have a draft of adopted regulations for Blowing Rock, including an STR ordinance, on file. As of this writing, the town has not begun to enforce the STR regulations.

c. City of Brevard, N.C., Code of Ordinances, Unified Dev. Ordinance § 3.34, https://www.cityofbrevard.com/DocumentCenter/View/1647/Ord-2017-08-Short-Term-Rental-Uses-PDF.

d. Town of Cornelius, N.C., Land Dev. Code § 6.2.45, https://www.cornelius.org/DocumentCenter/View/1616/CH-06-Uses-Permitted-With-Conditions?bidId=.

e. Lake Lure, N.C., Town Ordinances, Zoning Regulations § 92.042, https://www.egovlink.com/public_documents300/lakelure/published_documents/Town%20Ordinances/Chapter_92_Zoning_Regulations.pdf.

f. See *supra* section III.C.3 for a discussion of the evolution of Wilmington's STR ordinance.

less than $500,000 for each occurrence of bodily injury and property damage.[152] San Francisco requires the same, but it allows a host to opt out of showing proof of insurance coverage by certifying that he/she is only advertising the STR on platforms that automatically extend liability coverage to hosts.[153]

It is up to each local government to decide whether to ask for proof of liability coverage as part of the STR license application process. If a local government chooses not to mandate such a showing, it may opt to inform hosts that it is in their best interest to consider purchasing a commercial liability policy.

D. Making Revisions and Incorporating Feedback

It is good practice for local officials—e.g., planning and zoning officers, city or county attorneys, and other key local officials—to discuss draft ordinances in work sessions.[154] These officials will likely want to review a draft ordinance before it is scheduled for public hearing. It is important that the ordinance is legally defensible and that it aligns with community needs. Keep in mind that a poorly worded ordinance is nearly impossible to enforce. It may be advantageous for local officials to "play devil's advocate" by exploring ways the ordinance could be interpreted that are contrary to the drafters' intent.[155] Lastly, officials should consider allowing their governing boards to provide feedback on draft ordinances.

North Carolina courts have consistently mandated strict compliance with the procedural requirements that apply to the adoption of zoning amendments. The same holds true when it comes to the adoption of STR ordinances, as this type of zoning amendment also regulates land use. Thus, any local government in the state proposing an STR ordinance must provide public notice and hold a public hearing before adopting the ordinance. Local officials must also comply with the

---

152. Wilmington, N.C., Code of Ordinances, Land Dev. Code § 18-329(d), https://library.municode.com/nc/wilmington/codes/code_of_ordinances?nodeId=PTIIITECO_CH18LADECO_ART6SUDERE_DIVIPRCOSPUSPRACUSST_S18-329WHUSLOHOLOOOCBRBCBAIRFMXMSUMDI.

153. San Francisco Office of Short-Term Rentals, *supra* note 130 (the city's Office of Short-Term Rentals, in a question-and-answer section on its website, states that it is mandatory for STR hosts to "have property liability insurance in the amount of no less than $500,000, or provide proof that property liability coverage in an equal or higher amount is being provided by any and all hosting platforms through which you will rent your unit. Proof of liability insurance is not required if hosting activity is only handed by a platform (website) that already extends similar liability coverage").

154. *See* Carolyn Braun, *Drafting Clear Ordinances: Do's and Don'ts*, Planners Web (Apr. 17, 2010), http://plannersweb.com/2010/04/drafting-clear-ordinances-dos-and-donts/.

155. *Id.*

requirements set forth in G.S. 160A-383 (cities) and 153A-341 (counties) mandating the approval of a statement of consistency. G.S. 160A-383 provides as follows:[156]

> Prior to adopting or rejecting any zoning amendment, the governing board shall adopt one of the following statements which shall not be subject to judicial review:
>
> (1) A statement approving the zoning amendment and describing its consistency with an adopted comprehensive plan and explaining why the action taken is reasonable and in the public interest.
>
> (2) A statement rejecting the zoning amendment and describing its inconsistency with an adopted comprehensive plan and explaining why the action taken is reasonable and in the public interest.
>
> (3) A statement approving the zoning amendment and containing at least all of the following:
>
> a. A declaration that the approval is also deemed an amendment to the comprehensive plan. The governing board shall not require any additional request or application for amendment to the comprehensive plan.
>
> b. An explanation of the change in conditions the governing board took into account in amending the zoning ordinance to meet the development needs of the community.
>
> c. Why the action was reasonable and in the public interest.

The statement shall do more than restate the summary language contained in the statute.[157] If the statement of consistency is found to be insufficient, the zoning amendment may be void.[158]

---

156. *See also* Wally v. City of Kannapolis, 365 N.C. 449, 452 (2012) (quoting G.S. 160A-383).

157. Atkinson v. City of Charlotte, 235 N.C. App. 1, 4 (2014) (holding that the following statement failed to meet the statutory requirements of G.S. 160A-383: "This petition is found to be consistent with adopted policies and to be reasonable and in the public interest . . . .").

158. *Wally*, 365 N.C. at 453–54 (holding a zoning amendment to be void when the city council failed to approve a statement of reasonableness when adopting the amendment).

V. Oversight and Enforcement of Short-Term Rental Regulations

One could argue that the hard work doesn't really begin until after a local government passes a short-term rental (STR) ordinance. After all, rules will only be followed if they are enforced. Enforcement, for present purposes, can be separated into two categories: *registration compliance* and *operational compliance*.[159]

A. Registration Compliance

Registration compliance pertains to a local government's ability to effectively promote STR registration and identify unregistered properties. Some jurisdictions have made it unlawful to advertise an STR for rent unless the property's assigned registration/license number is clearly displayed in the advertisement.[160] This serves two purposes: it helps motivate hosts to register their properties and it allows local governments to more easily identify unregistered STRs. Despite registration requirements, local governments have found that hosts sometimes operate unregistered STRs.

Denver, Colo., began imposing fines on unlicensed STR operators in January 2017. The results of a recent audit conducted by the City and County of Denver's Auditor's Office showed that only 63 percent of the STR properties advertised for rent were associated with active STR licenses.[161] The auditors also found six instances of applicants sharing tax ID numbers for separate properties and forty-five instances where applicants applied for and received more than one STR license for properties located at the same address.[162] The auditors concluded that

---

159. Compliance actually operates at three levels: permit/registration compliance, code/operational compliance, and tax compliance; tax compliance is discussed *infra* section VIII. *See* STR Helper, *Compliance,* STR =HELPER.COM, https://strhelper.com/compliance/.

160. *See, e.g.,* CITY & CTY. OF DENVER, COLO., REVISED MUN. CODE § 33-49(d), https://www.denvergov.org/content/dam/denvergov/Portals/723/documents/STR%20Ordinance.pdf.

161. CITY & CTY. OF DENVER, OFFICE OF THE AUDITOR, AUDIT SERVS. DIV., AUDIT REPORT: DEP'T OF EXCISE & LICENSES & DEP'T OF FINANCE—TREASURY DIV., SHORT-TERM RENTAL ENFORCEMENT 10 (Dec. 2017), https://www.denvergov.org/content/dam/denvergov/Portals/741/documents/Audits_2017/ShortTermRentalEnforcement_December2017.pdf.

162. *Id.* at 19. *See also* Jesse Paul, *Lodger's Tax Collected on Denver Short-Term Rentals Nears $2 Million,* DENVER POST (Dec. 21, 2017), https://www.denverpost.com/2017/12/21/denver-short-term-rental-regulations/.

there was a flaw in the design of the STR application process and that the system should be configured so as to prohibit licensure that conflicts with existing STR regulations.[163] Perhaps easier said than done? The takeaway from the Denver audit is that local governments must carefully consider how to approach the registration of STRs. To increase compliance, it may be helpful to (1) keep the registration process simple, by, for example, allowing applicants to submit applications online, and (2) keep registration fees reasonable (remember: it is unlawful for a local government to profit from any of its business registration programs).

B. Operational Compliance

Local governments are often too busy (and frankly not in the best position) to monitor STR use. It is frequently neighboring property owners, and sometimes STR guests, who bring ordinance violations to the local government's attention. For example, if there are numerous guests at an STR property, a neighbor may file a complaint alleging that the STR owner has not abided by the maximum occupancy requirements in the local jurisdiction's ordinance. It may be helpful to establish a complaint process specific to STR violations *before* starting to enforce regulations. A local government can also opt to handle complaints in the same way it deals with other zoning enforcement matters.

Sonoma County, Cal., has enacted a detailed protocol designed to help streamline the STR complaint process. The Sonoma vacation rental ordinance directs any person registering an initial complaint to contact the responsible party named in the offending property's STR license application, the hope being that a resolution can be reached without involving the local government.[164] If the problem(s) persists, subsequent complaints are directed to the code enforcement office for investigation.[165] As part of its investigation, the code enforcement office will accept documentation of violations from STR neighbors in the form of photos and audio or video recordings. If the code enforcement office determines that a zoning or

---

163. Office of the Auditor, *supra* note 161, at 19.

164. Sonoma Cty., Cal., Code of Ordinances § 26-88-120g.1., https://sonomacounty.ca.gov/PRMD/Regulations/Vacation-and-Hosted-Rentals/Code-for-Vacation-Rentals/ ("Initial complaints on vacation rentals shall be directed to the certified property manager identified in the zoning permit or use permit, as applicable. The certified property manager shall be available 24 hours during all times when the property is rented and shall be available by phone during these hours.").

165. *Id.* ("If the issue reoccurs, the complaint will be addressed by [the county's Permit and Resource Management Division's] code enforcement section who may conduct an investigation to determine whether there was a violation of a zoning or use permit condition.").

use-permit condition violation has occurred, the host will be notified and possibly penalized in accordance with the county's code of ordinances.[166]

In establishing an STR complaint process, a local government may want to consider asking the following questions:

- How will initial complaints be registered?
- Will one local government staff member respond to all complaints?
- Who will conduct the investigations and decide whether a violation has occurred?
- How will STR hosts be notified of alleged violations?
- How long will hosts be given to respond to complaints with evidence of their own?
- Will hosts have the opportunity to demonstrate compliance with a regulation(s) for first violations and avoid penalties?
- Will the local government's budget allow for the hiring of additional staff to process and investigate complaints?

Once the local government has thought through every aspect of the STR grievance process, it will be in a better position to effectively resolve complaints and enforce new STR regulations.

C. Enforcement

In North Carolina, both cities and counties are vested with statutory authority to select enforcement methods for their ordinances, including the power to impose civil penalties or equitable remedies.[167] The enforcement method selected by a jurisdiction may be pursued when the relevant ordinance identifies it as a potential method of enforcement or when the enforcement method is detailed within a general "remedies" section of the jurisdiction's local code.[168] Under Section 14-4 of the North Carolina General Statutes, nearly all violations of city and county ordinances are classified as misdemeanors and carry a maximum fine of $500.

---

166. *Id.* ("[N]eighbor documentation consisting of photos, sound recordings and video may constitute proof of a violation. If code enforcement verifies that a zoning or use permit condition violation has occurred, a notice of violation may be issued, and a penalty may be imposed in accordance with Chapter 1 of the Sonoma County Code.").

167. G.S. 160A-175(c), (d) (cities); 153A-123(c), (d).

168. *See* Trey Allen, *Ordinance Enforcement Basics*, Coates' Canons: NC Loc. Gov't L. blog (Feb. 1, 2016), https://canons.sog.unc.edu/ordinance-enforcement-basics/ ("Local governments have the ability to enforce their ordinances through any or all of several civil measures, including civil penalties and court orders directing offenders to comply with particular ordinances.").

No city/county ordinance violation penalty can exceed $50 unless the ordinance expressly permits it.

While there is no statutory maximum for civil penalties related to ordinance violations,[169] it is important to bear in mind that the penalty must not be grossly disproportionate to the corresponding offense and should not be exceptionally more substantial compared with other civil penalties imposed by the jurisdiction.[170] An ordinance may specify that each day's continuing violation is a separate and distinct offense, which will quickly result in mounting civil penalties. For example, the City of Asheville and the Town of Blowing Rock both impose a $500-per-day fine on hosts who violate each jurisdiction's short-term rental ordinance.[171] One Asheville resident made headlines for racking up nearly $1 million in fines for operating an STR in a prohibited zoning district.[172]

Some cities nationwide have chosen to enact a graduated scale of civil fines for STR ordinance violations. This method may be useful when STRs are an allowed use subject to certain operational regulations (e.g., occupancy limitations, noise or parking restrictions). In Savannah, Ga., a host will be fined $500 for the first STR ordinance violation. However, if, within a twelve-month period, the host accrues additional violations, the fines increase to $750 for a second violation, $1,000 for a third, and, finally, the host may have his or her STR certificate revoked.[173] Similarly, in Boulder, Colo., after notice and an opportunity for a quasi-judicial hearing have been extended to an STR host, the city may impose a civil penalty of $500 for the first violation of an ordinance provision, $750 for a second violation of the same provision, and $1,000 for a third violation. If another provision is violated by the host, the fines are $150 for the first violation, $300 for the second, and $1,000 for the third.[174]

---

169. *See* David M. Lawrence, *Are There Limits on the Size of Penalties to Enforce Local Government Ordinances?*, Loc. Gov't L. Bull. No. 128, at 3 (July 2012), https://www.sog.unc.edu/sites/www.sog.unc.edu/files/reports/lglb128.pdf.

170. *Id.*; *see also* U.S. Const. art. VII.

171. Asheville, N.C., Code § 7-18-2(b)(1)c., https://library.municode.com/nc/asheville/codes/code_of_ordinances?nodeId=PTIICOOR_CH7DE_ARTXVIIIEN_S7-18-2PEVI; Blowing Rock, N.C., Town Code, Land Use Ordinance § 16-7.7, http://www.townofblowingrocknc.gov/home/showdocument?id=256.

172. Tim Waller, *Asheville Man Racked Up a Million Dollars in Airbnb Fines*, WYFF4.com (Oct. 8, 2018), https://www.wyff4.com/article/asheville-man-racked-up-a-million-dollars-in-airbnb-fines/23656931.

173. Savannah, Ga., Code of Ordinances §§ 8-10017(e), (b), respectively, https://library.municode.com/ga/savannah/codes/code_of_ordinances?nodeId=DIVIICOGEOR_PT8PLREDE_CH11SHRMVARE_S8-11017SHRMVAREPR.

174. Boulder, Colo., Mun. Code § 10-3-16(a)(1), https://library.municode.com/co/boulder/codes/municipal_code?nodeId=TIT10ST_CH3RELI_10-3-16ADRE .

Quiz: Ordinance Violation Fees

Facts: A local government plans to charge $200 for an initial violation of its STR ordinance, $350 for a second violation, and $500 for a third. The jurisdiction will revoke the violator's STR permit for any additional violations. Is this allowed?

Answer: Yes. A local government may set a graduated scale of fines, use a flat-fee approach, or rely on the enforcement provisions already included in its UDO. Fines for violations are not mandatory. Alternatively, a local government may simply revoke a violator's permit after "three strikes."

In lieu of, or in addition to, collecting civil penalties for STR ordinance violations, a local government may allow for equitable remedies, such as permit revocation.[175] Nashville, Tenn., for example, does not impose civil penalties on STR ordinance violators on a per-complaint basis. Instead, once there have been three violations of the ordinance within a twelve-month period, the violator's STR permit may be revoked and cannot be renewed for one year.[176]

A local government is not required to craft a new enforcement provision for STR ordinances. The easiest approach may be to cite directly to relevant provisions already set forth in the jurisdiction's zoning unified development ordinance (UDO). (See the sample ordinance in Appendix A.)

D. Penalties

A civil penalty action is one "in the nature of debt."[177] This means that a violator of an ordinance with a civil penalty provision owes a debt to his or her city or county.[178] A local government may initiate an action to collect on the debt in either district or superior court.[179] It may also pursue a judgment in small claims court

175. *See, e.g.*, G.S. 160A-175(d) (cities); 153A-123(d) (counties).

176. Code of Metro. Gov't of Nashville & Davidson Cty., Tenn., § 17.16.250E.4.l.ii, https://library.municode.com/tn/metro_government_of_nashville_and_davidson_county/codes/code_of_ordinances?nodeId=CD_TIT17ZO_CH17.16LAUSDEST_ARTIVUSPEACA_17.16.250REACUS.

177. Allen, *supra* note 168.

178. *Id.*

179. *Id.*; *see also* Asheville, N.C., Code § 7-18-4, https://library.municode.com/nc/asheville/codes/code_of_ordinances?nodeId=PTIICOOR_CH7DE_ARTXVIIIEN_S7-18-4ACRECIPEACINCRPR (authorizing the city attorney to institute a civil action against any person who neglects to pay a civil penalty within the time specified in the citation issued to the person).

when the civil penalty is small enough to qualify. The Setoff Debt Collection Act, outlined in Chapter105A of the North Carolina General Statutes, offers an alternative to litigation for local governments seeking to collect civil penalties in excess of $50.[180] The bottom line is that local governments have authority to enforce their civil ordinances, including STR ordinances.

E. Compliance Monitoring

Recognizing that local governments may struggle both with drafting STR regulations and with enforcing them, at least two software companies, Host Compliance[181] and STR Helper,[182] offer services to assist local governments with any compliance, registration, or licensing-related needs.[183] New Hanover County, N.C., has contracted with STR Helper in an effort to streamline the collection of occupancy taxes. Under the arrangement, property owners can pay these taxes using STR Helper's online payment portal.[184] Blowing Rock, N.C., is also using STR Helper to track the location of STRs and for its occupancy tax–collection services.[185]

One possible downside to contracting with STR Helper, Host Compliance, or another monitoring company is that the services offered by these businesses can be pricey. While it may be tempting for a jurisdiction to share the cost of compliance monitoring with its tourism development authority (TDA), nearly all local occupancy tax bills require that tax proceeds be spent to "promote travel and tourism" (two-thirds of net tax proceeds) or for "tourism-related expenditures"

---

180. G.S. Ch. 105A; *see also* Allen, *supra* note 168.

181. The address for the Host Compliance website is https://hostcompliance.com/.

182. The address for the STR Helper website is https://strhelper.com/.

183. Host Compliance states that its "software platform can help manage all of the registration, permitting, address identification, compliance monitoring, enforcement, outreach, tax collection and complaint processes so city staff can focus on higher value-added activities." Host Compliance, *supra* note 181. STR Helper states that it "is a full-fledged end-to-end software solution that allows local governments to manage compliance, registration, licensing, communications, and complaints regarding the short-term rentals in their area." STR Helper, *supra* note 182.

184. Tim Buckland, *New Hanover to Launch Program to Track Short-Term Rentals*, Star News Online (May 18, 2018), https://www.starnewsonline.com/news/20180518/new-hanover-to-launch-program-to-track-short-term-rentals ("Beginning in July, the county will simultaneously launch software that will track short-term rental use and provide a simpler way for short-term rental owners to pay room-occupancy taxes.").

185. Thomas Sherrill, *Blowing Rock to Combat Short-Term Rental Issue with Software Tracker*, Blowing Rocket (Apr. 5, 2018), https://www.wataugademocrat.com/blowingrocket/blowing-rock-to-combat-short-term-rental-issue-with-software/article_b434e966-4b47-5073-b259-28ee2e7e9729.html.

(one-third).[186] It is unclear whether the cost of compliance monitoring would qualify as a "tourism-related expenditure." In the authors' opinion, it may not.

VI. Next Steps

For local governments interested in revising their local codes to reach and regulate short-term rental properties (STRs), now is a good time to begin that process. The questions below should help jump-start regulation efforts.

- Why does our city/county want to regulate STRs?
- Where in the city-county will STRs be allowed?
- Who will be allowed to apply for an STR permit (e.g., property owner, lessee)?
- What will the permit application process entail?
- What is a reasonable STR registration fee?
- How will our city/county verify that a permit applicant has authority to rent the property at issue?
- Will the application process require an in-person inspection or a self-inspection checklist?
- Will there be an occupancy cap on STRs?
- What information will be necessary to include in online advertisements of STR rentals?
- How will our city/county enforce the new STR ordinance?
- How will our city/county handle the rental of *accessory dwelling units* (i.e., non-STR units attached to/on the same grounds as STR units)?
- Which city/county employee(s) will oversee STR registration and compliance?

---

186. *See* N.C. GEN. ASSEMB., RESEARCH DIV., GUIDELINES FOR OCCUPANCY TAX LEGISLATION (revised Sept. 13, 2013) (hereinafter LEGISLATIVE GUIDELINES), reproduced in Appendix B. For additional discussion of TDAs, including issues relating to expenditures, see section X, *infra*.

VII. Short-Term Rentals and Occupancy Taxes

A. Background

North Carolina's beaches and mountains have drawn tourists from across the country for well over 100 years.[187] Tourists have long paid sales taxes on the cost of their rental accommodations, and some of the revenue generated by these taxes is shared with local governments.[188] However, it was not until 1983 that the North Carolina General Assembly began to grant local governments authority to levy their own occupancy taxes on the cost of short-term rentals such as hotels, bed and breakfast inns, and vacation homes.[189] Today, roughly eighty counties and eighty municipalities in the state levy occupancy taxes ranging from 1 percent to 8 percent.[190] These taxes generate more than $270 million in local government revenue each year,[191] most of which must be spent on promoting local tourism.[192] See Table 3, *infra*, for a summary of these figures and Appendix B for a complete list of counties and towns that levy occupancy taxes and their rates as of 2017.

---

187. *See, e.g.*, Omni Hotels & Resorts, *The Grove Park Inn Story*, OMNIHOTELS.COM, https://www.omnihotels.com/hotels/asheville-grove-park/property-details/history (noting, among other things, that Asheville's historic Grove Park Inn opened its doors in 1913); First Colony Inn, *Our History: Nags Head and the First Colony Inn*, FIRSTCOLONYINN.COM, https://www.firstcolonyinn.com/our-history (the First Colony Inn in Nags Head opened in 1838).

188. The North Carolina Sales and Use Tax Act became law in 1957. G.S. 105-164.1. Sales taxes apply to "accommodation rentals" thanks to G.S. 105-164.4(a)(3) and -164.4F. As of the date of this writing, the general sales tax rate that applies to accommodation rentals in North Carolina is 4.75 percent, the revenue from which remains with the state. G.S. 105-164.4(a). Counties are authorized to levy up to an additional 2.25 percent of local sales tax, the proceeds of which are shared among the county of origin and the municipalities in that county on either a per capita or ad valorem basis. G.S. 105-472. Local sales taxes and their distribution are explained in detail in this blog post by School of Government faculty member Kara Millonzi: https://canons.sog.unc.edu/local-sales-and-use-tax-changes/.

189. *See* LEGISLATIVE GUIDELINES, *supra* note 186.

190. The North Carolina Department of Revenue releases a report each year that lists the counties and municipalities that levy occupancy taxes as well as their rates and total collections. *See* N.C. DEP'T OF REVENUE, OCCUPANCY TAX COLLECTIONS REPORT FISCAL YEAR 2016–2017 (hereinafter OCCUPANCY TAX COLLECTIONS 2017). Another resource for North Carolina occupancy tax information is a list, maintained and regularly updated by the legislative research staff at the General Assembly, of all occupancy tax local bills. *See* N.C. DEP'T OF REVENUE, OCCUPANCY TAX OVERVIEW, cited in full, *supra* note 6.

191. OCCUPANCY TAX COLLECTIONS 2017.

192. *See* section VIII, *infra*, for more details on how occupancy tax revenues may be used by local governments.

Table 3. North Carolina Occupancy Tax Summary 2017

Number of Counties Levying Occupancy Taxes	Total County Occupancy Tax Revenue	Number of Municipalities Levying Occupancy Taxes	Total Municipal Occupancy Tax Revenue
81*	$228 million	80**	$44 million

Source: Occupancy Tax Collections 2017, n.4.
*Three counties (Caswell, Iredell, and Wilkes) are authorized to levy occupancy taxes but do not currently do so.
**Fifteen municipalities (Crossnore, Elk Park, Grandfather Village, Linville, Newland, Sugar Mountain, Yanceyville, Coolemee, Cramerton, Lowell, McAdenville, Ranio, Carrboro, Hillsborough, and Elizabeth City) are authorized to levy occupancy taxes but do not do so.

This section discusses the details behind local occupancy taxes, including the levy process, the scope of this type of tax, collection remedies, and the use of proceeds.

B. Local Occupancy Tax Bills

There is no general authorization for local occupancy taxes in North Carolina. The only local governments that may levy these taxes are those that have been granted authority to do so by the General Assembly via local acts.[193] As mentioned above, more than two-thirds of the state's 100 counties and nearly 100 of the state's 550+ municipalities have received authority to levy occupancy taxes and have exercised that authority.[194]

193. This differs from "home rule" states, which accord local governments much more authority to act without the need for legislation. *See* Nat'l League of Cities, *Cities 101—Delegation of Power*, NLC.org (Dec. 13, 2016), https://www.nlc.org/resource/cities-101-delegation-of-power ("Home rule is a delegation of power from the state to its sub-units of governments (including counties, municipalities, towns or townships or villages)." That power is limited to specific fields, and subject to constant judicial interpretation, but home rule creates local autonomy and limits the degree of state interference in local affairs); Cmty. Envtl. Legal Def. Fund, *Home Rule*, CELDF.org, https://celdf.org/law-library/local-law-center/home-rule/ (noting that "(f)orty-three states in the U.S. either constitutionally or statutorily allow for Municipal Home Rule"). As our School of Government colleague Frayda Bluestein explained in a 2012 blog post, North Carolina is not a home rule state. Frayda Bluestein, *Is North Carolina a Dillon's Rule State?*, Coates' Canons: NC Loc. Gov't L. blog (Oct. 24, 2012), https://canons.sog.unc.edu/is-north-carolina-a-dillons-rule-state/.

194. *See* Occupancy Tax Collections 2017.

Table 4. Top Ten County and Top Ten Municipal Occupancy Tax Collections 2017

County	Occupancy Tax Collections (in Millions)	Municipality	Occupancy Tax Collections (in Millions)
Mecklenburg	$56.4	Greensboro	$5.0
Dare	$28.2	Wilmington	$3.6
Wake	$24.6	Ocean Isle Beach	$2.4
Buncombe	$21.0	Hickory	$1.9
Durham	$12.8	Holden Beach	$1.9
Currituck	$11.5	Boone	$1.8
Carteret	$7.0	Lumberton	$1.5
Cumberland	$6.2	Oak Island	$1.4
Guilford	$5.7	Chapel Hill	$1.1
New Hanover	$5.7	Wrightsville Beach	$1.1

Source: Occupancy Tax Collections 2017.

The North Carolina General Statutes contain "boilerplate" administrative provisions for local occupancy taxes (G.S. 153A-155 for counties and 160A-215 for cities; both sections are reproduced in Appendix C). The General Assembly has taken additional steps to make these taxes more uniform across the state by adopting guidelines (uniform provisions) for local occupancy tax bills.[195]

Most local occupancy taxes either mirror these provisions or specifically adopt them.[196] For example, every local act specifies a maximum occupancy tax rate and the permitted uses of tax proceeds. But some local acts still contain unique provisions and requirements for particular jurisdictions.[197] With that in mind, when questions about a jurisdiction's occupancy tax arises, it is important to first consult that jurisdiction's local act.

195. Legislative Guidelines, *supra* note 186.

196. In 2013, the General Assembly enacted S.L. 2013-414 in an effort to increase uniformity among local occupancy taxes. This law amended approximately fifteen local acts to make them conform to the uniform provisions. Despite the legislature's standardization efforts, there are a few local acts that are outliers and that contain significant variations in the authorizing language.

197. For example, one of Wake County's local bills, S.L. 1995-458, creates successor liability for occupancy taxes by adopting the sales-tax successor liability provision found in G.S. 105-164.38(b). See section VIII, *infra*, for more on liability for local occupancy taxes.

A local government that does not levy occupancy taxes but is interested in doing so would need to work with its state legislators to introduce a local bill granting it that authority. Most legislative sessions produce several bills that create or expand occupancy tax authority for local governments.[198]

The basic process for a local government to begin levying an occupancy tax is as follows:

1. Obtain authorization through a local bill from the General Assembly.
2. Adopt a resolution levying an occupancy tax after public hearing.
3. Create a Tourism Development Authority (TDA).
4. Collect taxes and distribute proceeds to the TDA for use on tourism-related expenditures. (Sections X and VIII, *infra*, discuss TDAs and the use of occupancy taxes.)

The standard procedure for levying an occupancy tax mandated by G.S. 153A-155 and 160A-215 requires a resolution adopted after a public hearing for which the local government's governing board provided at least ten days' advance notice to the public. Alternatively, the local government could act through an ordinance, which requires more procedural formality than does a resolution.[199] In its resolution or ordinance, the local governing board will set the jurisdiction's effective tax rate, in an amount up to the maximum rate specified in the relevant local bill. That occupancy tax rate continues in effect until it is changed or repealed by the board or by the General Assembly. Unlike property taxes, the occupancy tax does not need to be levied annually.[200]

1. The Occupancy Tax Rate

Each local government that levies an occupancy tax sets its own rate, up to the maximum rate specified in the local bill authorizing the tax. A local government that has been granted occupancy tax authorization is free to change its rate whenever it desires, so long as that rate does not exceed the relevant maximum rate.

---

198. See, for example, S.L. 2017-202 (affecting occupancy taxes in nine counties and towns). During the 2015–2016 legislative session, five bills touched on local occupancy taxes: S.L. 2015-102, 2015-128, 2015-255, 2015-256, and 2016-65.

199. School of Government faculty member Frayda Bluestein describes the differences between resolutions and ordinances in these two posts from the School's *Coates' Canons: NC Local Government Law* blog: *Now Therefore, Be it Resolved . . .* (Mar. 13, 2013), https://canons.sog.unc.edu/now-therefore-be-it-resolved/, and *Voting Rules for Adopting Ordinances* (Jan. 21, 2015), https://canons.sog.unc.edu/voting-rules-for-adopting-ordinances/.

200. Property taxes must be levied annually in the budget ordinance, as required by the Local Government Budget and Fiscal Control Act, G.S. Chapter 159, Article 3.

Quiz: Changes to the Occupancy Tax Rate

Question: Does a local government need approval from the General Assembly to change its occupancy tax rate?

Answer: No. Once the General Assembly passes a local bill that authorizes a local government to levy an occupancy tax up to a certain rate, the local government may set and later change its rate at any time, so long as that rate does not exceed the maximum established by its local bill.

Most local bills initially set the maximum rate at 3 percent, with some local governments receiving subsequent authorization to raise their rates up to 6 percent.[201] Brunswick County appears to be subject to the lowest cap, with a rate that is limited to 1 percent.[202] The combined Mecklenburg County/Charlotte occupancy tax rate cap of 8 is the highest in the state and the only one above 6 percent.[203] A list of tax rates for all North Carolina local governments that levy occupancy taxes is provided in Appendix D.

---

201. The General Assembly's *Guidelines for Occupancy Tax Legislation* (LEGISLATIVE GUIDELINES), cited in full *supra* note 186 and reproduced in Appendix B, state that "[t]he county tax rate cannot exceed 6% and the city tax rate, when combined with the county rate, cannot exceed 6%." These guidelines are recommendations and not binding law. That said, the General Assembly has stuck by the guidelines and, with the exception of Mecklenburg County/Charlotte's 8 percent occupancy tax, has not authorized any county/municipal occupancy taxes that, in the aggregate, exceed 6 percent. In Surry County and Watauga County, both the counties and several of their municipalities have authority to levy occupancy taxes of up to 6 percent. But the county authority in both instances covers only unincorporated areas, meaning that the aggregate occupancy tax never exceeds 6 percent in either county. *See* S.L. 2009-112 (Surry County occupancy tax) *and* S.L. 2005-197 (Watauga County occupancy tax). Assuming the General Assembly continues to honor the *Legislative Guidelines* in future sessions, a municipality will effectively be prevented from obtaining occupancy tax authority if its county already levies an occupancy tax of 6 percent.

202. OCCUPANCY TAX COLLECTIONS 2017, *supra* note 190.

203. This tax actually covers Mecklenburg County and the cities of Charlotte, Cornelius, Davidson, Huntersville, Matthews, Mint Hill, and Pineville. The extra 2 percent of tax above the standard 6 percent cap was authorized in 2005 to help finance the NASCAR Hall of Fame in downtown Charlotte. *See* S.L. 1983-908, S.L. 1989-821, S.L. 2001-402, S.L. 2005-68, S.L. 2009-445, S.L. 2012-194, S.L. 2013-26.

2. Taxable Accommodations

Under G.S. 153A-155(b) and 160A-215(b), local occupancy taxes apply to the same transactions that are subject to state sales taxes on accommodations mandated by G.S. 105-164.4(a)(3). This last statute references G.S. 105-164.4F, which addresses taxable accommodation rentals in detail.[204]

G.S. 105-164.4F(a)(1) defines "accommodation" as "[a] hotel room, a motel room, a residence, a cottage, or a similar lodging facility for occupancy by an individual." This definition is seemingly broad enough to cover, for tax purposes, any type of structure that is rented for temporary residential use, be it a houseboat, a tent, a yurt,[205] a caboose,[206] or even a remote lighthouse station.[207] But parking spots for recreational vehicles, campsites, boat slips, and other rental properties that do not include any type of residential structures would **not** be subject to sales or local occupancy taxes based on the definition of "accommodation" found in G.S. 105-164.4F.

This statute explicitly excludes from sales and occupancy taxes three types of accommodation rentals:

"(1) A private residence, cottage, or similar accommodation that is rented for fewer than 15 days in a calendar year other than a private residence, cottage, or similar accommodation listed with a real estate broker or agent.
(2) An accommodation supplied to the same person for a period of 90 or more continuous days.
(3) An accommodation arranged or provided to a person by a school, camp, or similar entity where a tuition or fee is charged to the person for enrollment in the school, camp, or similar entity."[208]

Local governments do not have the authority to create additional exemptions from their occupancy taxes beyond these three statutory exemptions. In 2013,

---

204. G.S. 105-164.4F is reproduced in Appendix C.

205. *See* Glamping Hub, *Luxury Yurt Camping Near Lake Nantahala in National Forest of North Carolina*, GLAMPINGHUB.COM, https://glampinghub.com/unitedstatesofamerica/southeast/northcarolina/topton/nantahala-yurt-camping-north-carolina/.

206. *See* Glamping Hub, *Glamping Caboose Rental Perfect for Families Near Clyde, North Carolina*, GLAMPINGHUB.COM, https://glampinghub.com/unitedstatesofamerica/southeast/northcarolina/clyde/glamping-clyde-north-carolina/.

207. *See* Frying Pan Tower, *Welcome to Frying Pan Tower*, FPTOWER.COM, www.fptower.com (describing this destination spot, a former U.S. Coast Guard light station thirty-four miles off the coast of Bald Head Island, North Carolina, which is now a privately owned bed and breakfast inn).

208. G.S. 105-164.4F(e).

Quiz: Taxability of Specific Accommodations

Question: Which of the following rentals are subject to occupancy taxes?

(a) A hotel room rented to a private nonprofit hurricane relief agency for sixty days

(b) A house listed with a rental agency and rented during the two weeks of the U.S. Open golf tournament

(c) A cabin owned by the Boy Scouts of America rented to a family for a week

(d) All of the above

Answer: (d). All of these rentals are taxable, assuming that the occupancy tax in question conforms with the three standard statutory exemptions discussed above.

the General Assembly passed a law that eliminated additional exemptions found in many older local occupancy tax bills, including exemptions for nonprofits that rent out accommodations and for businesses that rent out fewer than five units.[209] But not all unique local exemptions were eliminated. There are still several local occupancy tax bills that include the nonprofit exemption or other exemptions not listed in G.S. 105-164.4F.[210] A jurisdiction's tax officials should refer to their specific local occupancy tax bill to determine whether their tax is limited to the three exemptions listed in G.S. 105-164.4F or if other exemptions remain in effect in their locality.

The three statutory occupancy tax exemptions are discussed in greater detail in the subsections below.

209. S.L. 2013-414.

210. For example, both Wake and Orange counties still exempt accommodations "furnished by nonprofit charitable, educational, benevolent, or religious organizations when furnished in furtherance of their nonprofit purpose." S.L. 1991-392 (Orange County) and S.L. 1991-594, Sec. 4 (Wake County). It's unclear exactly what it means for rental property to be made available in "furtherance of [a] nonprofit purpose." For property tax purposes, any rental property owned by a nonprofit and rented out to the general public at market rates would be considered to be used for a commercial purpose rather than a nonprofit purpose and, therefore, would be taxable. But under Orange County's and Wake County's occupancy tax exemptions, it seems that rental property with some connection to a nonprofit's exempt activities (cabins made available for rent at a YMCA campground, for example) would be exempt from taxation, even if the nonprofit is charging market rates and making the rentals available to the general public.

a. Occasional Rental of Private Residence

When a property owner rents his or her private residence for fewer than fifteen days per calendar year, under G.S. 105-164.4F(e)(1), the monies derived from the rental activity are not subject to the occupancy tax. For example, a property owner who made her beach house available for rental the last two weeks of July every year would not be subject to occupancy tax on those rentals. Likewise, a property owner who wants to rent out his house only during a short-term event such as a golf tournament or wine festival could qualify for this exemption.[211]

This exception does not apply, however, to any residence that is listed with a rental agent, regardless of the number of days the property is actually rented.[212] Online STR platforms such as Airbnb and Vacation Rentals by Owner (VRBO) likely do not qualify as rental agents for purposes of this exemption. If a rental is made through an online STR platform, responsibility for occupancy taxes on that rental may shift from the property owner to the online STR platform. (See *infra* section VIII.B.1 for more on this topic.)

The N.C. Department of Revenue interprets the residential rental exemption to cover only property that is not "generally or routinely" made available for rental.[213] Under this interpretation, if a property owner is regularly trying to rent out a property by himself or herself or through an online STR platform, then all rentals of that property are subject to occupancy taxes, even if the property is rented for fewer than fifteen days total in a calendar year.[214] Of course, as mentioned above, if the property is listed with a real estate agent, then all rental income is taxable regardless of how long the property is made available.

This exemption should not be read to mean that the first fifteen days for which a property is rented are automatically exempt from occupancy taxes. The exemp-

---

211. But, under this same statutory subsection, if the property is listed with a broker or agent for such event-specific rentals, the rentals would be subject to occupancy taxes regardless of the length of the rental. The brokers-or-agents exception to the fifteen-day exemption was enacted in 2014, in large part to help Moore County capture occupancy taxes on luxury homes rented out during the 2014 U.S. Open golf tournament at the Pinehurst golf resort. S.L. 2014-3, § 8.1(b). *See also* Edmundson CPA, PLLC, *NC Welcomes US Open with New Taxes*, NCCPA.COM, (June 5, 2014), https://www.nccpa.com/nc-welcomes-us-open-with-new-taxes/.

212. G.S. 105-164.4F(e)(1). Subsection (d) of this same statute defines "rental agent" as "a person who, by written contract, agrees to be the rental agent for the provider of an accommodation."

213. N.C. DEP'T OF REVENUE, SALES & USE TAX DIV., SALES & USE TAX TECHNICAL BULLETINS § 27-1(D) (Jan. 15, 2009) (hereinafter SALES & USE TAX TECHNICAL BULLETINS), https://files.nc.gov/ncdor/documents/files/sales_and_use_tax_combined_bulletins_1.pdf. If an accommodation rental is subject to sales taxes, it also subject to local occupancy taxes unless a unique local occupancy tax exemption applies.

214. *Id.*

tion will apply only if the property owner intends to limit rentals to fewer than fifteen days in a year. If a property owner intends to make the property available for rental for any period of time in excess of fourteen days, then occupancy taxes should begin with the very first rental of that property.

This exemption should also not be interpreted to allow property owners to rent their residences for up to fifteen days when local law otherwise prohibits them from doing so. For example, if a municipality has banned short-term rentals from residentially-zoned districts, property owners in those districts may not lawfully rent a property for any amount of days. (See section IV, *supra*, for more on local regulation of STRs.)

b. Long-Term Rental

If the same accommodation is rented to the same person for ninety or more consecutive days, under G.S. 105-164.4F(e)(2), that rental is not subject to occupancy taxes. In some cases, the duration of the tenant's stay may be not be determined until after the tenant has paid for a portion of the stay. If the property owner has already remitted occupancy taxes on the rental to the taxing unit and thereafter the rental period unexpectedly extends beyond ninety days, the owner may claim a refund for any taxes paid on the rental. The property owner should return that tax refund to the tenant, the party who originally paid the occupancy taxes as part of the bill for the accommodation rental.[215] (See section IX.A, *infra*, for more on occupancy tax refunds.)

Consider a family that rents a beach house for two summer months, June and July. The owner of that property must collect and remit taxes on that rental. If the family decides to extend the rental through the end of August, the rental would now be greater than eighty-nine continuous days. The property owner would not need to collect taxes for the August rent and may seek a refund from the taxing unit of the taxes paid on the rental for June and July.

A corporation, partnership, or government is considered a person for purposes of the long-term rental exemption.[216] As a result, if a hotel room is rented to one

---

215. Note that it is not the job of the taxing unit to ensure that owners provide refunds to tenants in these situations. The taxing unit fulfills its obligation by refunding the property owner, who is then obligated to reimburse the tenant.

216. G.S. 105-164.3, which defines the terms used in all of the General Statutes' sales tax provisions, including G.S. 105-164.4, adopts the definition of "person" set out in G.S. 105-228.90(b)(5). Under this definition, a "person" is "[a]n individual, a fiduciary, a firm, an association, a partnership, a limited liability company, a corporation, a unit of government, or another group acting as a unit." Because local occupancy tax provisions incorporate G.S. 105-164.4, they also incorporate the definitions that apply to that section, including this expansive definition of the term "person."

Quiz: Charges Subject to Occupancy Taxes

Facts: Wanda Wolfpack is charged the following for her one-week beach house rental: $1,500 for rent, a $150 VRBO reservation fee, a $100 security damage waiver, and a $200 optional beach club membership. What is the total amount subject to occupancy taxes?

(a) $1,500

(b) $1,650

(c) $1,750

(d) $1,950

Answer: (c). The only charge that is not subject to occupancy taxes is the $200 beach club membership.

organization for ninety or more consecutive days, that rental is exempt from occupancy taxes, even if different employees or agents of that organization use the room during the rental period. For example, assume that an airline reserves multiple hotel rooms near an airport for six months at a time for use by different flight crews. Those hotel room rentals would be exempt from occupancy taxes, despite the fact that different people were staying in the rooms on different days.

c. *School, Camp, and Hospital Accommodations*

Occupancy taxes do not apply to any accommodation that is provided in connection with a tenant's enrollment or participation in a school, camp, or similar activity. For example, children attending a residential summer camp are not charged occupancy taxes for the costs of their bunks. Similarly, hospitals and medical clinics providing in-patient care are not charged occupancy taxes for the costs of their rooms.[217]

3. Rentals to Government Employees

Some accommodation rentals made to governments and their employees may be exempt from local occupancy taxes, depending on the type of government involved and the method of payment used. See Table 5, *infra*.

217. *See* email from Ginny C. Upchurch, Director, N.C. Dep't of Revenue, Sales & Use Tax Div., to the authors (Jan. 14, 2018) (on file with authors) ("Generally speaking, a hospital is not in the business of providing accommodations to patients, as they are providing medical care/treatment to patients. Hospital rooms where a patient stays while undergoing medical care/treatment are not subject to tax as an accommodation.").

Table 5. Occupancy Taxes and Rentals by Government Workers

Type of Government Employee	Rental Exempt from Occupancy Taxes?
Federal	Yes, if rental is paid for using government-issued credit card that is billed directly to the federal government[a]
Foreign Diplomat	Yes, if in possession of a tax-exemption card issued by the U.S. Department of State that does not specifically exclude occupancy taxes[b]
State	No[c]
City or County or Regional Authority	No[d]

a. Sales & Use Tax Technical Bulletins § 37-1(A). *See also* U.S. Gen. Servs. Admin., *State Tax Exemption Information for Government Charge Cards*, GSA.gov, https://www.gsa.gov/travel/plan-book/state-tax-exemption-information-for-government-charge-cards.

b. *See* U.S. Dep't of State, *Sales Tax Exemption*, State.gov, https://www.state.gov/ofm/tax/sales/.

c. Sales & Use Tax Bulletins § 18-2(D)(4).

d. *Id.* § 18-1(A)(1).

4. Taxable Rental Charges

Occupancy taxes apply to the cost of the accommodation rental and to other mandatory charges related to that rental, such as early or late departure fees, extra person charges, cleaning fees, and pet fees. Table 6, *infra*, shows the complete list of taxable fees identified by the N.C. Department of Revenue (DOR), as well as some examples of charges that should not be subject to local occupancy taxes.[218]

The DOR's list of taxable charges includes security deposits, which are usually returned, at least in part, to guests at the end of their stays. If a security deposit is refunded (in part or in total) to a guest, then the hotel/property owner should also return to the guest any occupancy taxes charged on that security deposit.

As Table 6, *infra*, illustrates, charges for the optional use of tangible personal property on-site or for various other services are not subject to occupancy taxes.[219]

218. North Carolina Department of Revenue: https://files.nc.gov/ncdor/documents/important-notices/impnotice0108.pdf.

219. Such charges may be subject to sales and use taxes, however. *See supra* section VII.B.2.

Table 6. Taxable and Non-Taxable Rental Charges

Charges Subject to Occupancy Taxes

Credit card fees

Damage fees

Early/late departure fees

- Extra person charges
- In-room safe rentals
- Inspection fees
- Linen fees
- Maid/cleaning fees
- "Peace of mind" fees (similar to insurance but provided by hotels or rental agencies rather than by third-party carriers)
- Pet fees (incurred by guests who have pets traveling with them)
- Reservation fees (also referred to as a handling, processing, or administrative fees)
- Security deposits
- Smoking fees
- Transfer fees (for changing to a different room or unit or to a different date)
- Tentative reservation fees (e.g., for priority reservations in subsequent years)
- Charges for cribs and roll-away beds
- Charges for microwave ovens and refrigerators

Charges NOT Subject to Occupancy Taxes

Rentals of video tapes, DVDs, and related video equipment

Rentals of beach equipment, such as chairs, toys, and umbrellas

Rentals of recreational equipment, such as skis, surf boards, and snorkeling equipment

Rentals of audio-visual equipment

In summary, all mandatory charges that are directly related to the use and occupancy of the rental accommodation are subject to occupancy taxes, but voluntary charges relating to optional rentals or services that may enhance a travel experience are not.[220]

220. If charges subject to the occupancy tax are bundled with charges not subject to the occupancy tax in such a manner that the customer pays only a single price, then the taxable portion of that price may be determined either through the procedures outlined in G.S. 105-164.4D, if applicable, or by using a "reasonable allocation" of pricing based on the operator's accounting records. G.S. 153A-155(c), 160A-215(c).

VIII. Liability for Occupancy Taxes

There are three different parties who may be held liable for collecting occupancy taxes from tenants and for remitting (in other words, paying) those tax receipts to the appropriate local governments.

- **Retailers**—any person or business entity that provides an accommodation that is offered for lease or rent.[221] Retailers include operators of hotels, motels, and bed and breakfast inns, as well as owners of short-term vacation rentals.
- **Facilitators**—any person or business entity (1) that contracts with the provider of an accommodation in order to market the accommodation and (2) that may accept payment for the rental.[222] Facilitators include on-line rental listing services such as Airbnb and HomeAway.
- **Rental Agents**—includes real estate brokers and other persons who are engaged in the business of property management, including local real estate firms that manage vacation rentals for homeowners.[223]

A. Retailer Liability

Liability for property taxes on accommodation rentals normally rests with the retailer, meaning the owner or operator of the accommodation. For example, if the Tar Heel Town Motel does not file a county occupancy tax return or pay any county occupancy taxes, the county may use its enforced collection remedies for those delinquent taxes against the owner of that motel. (See section VIII.D, *infra*, for more details about those collection remedies.)

But changes to North Carolina's tax provisions in recent years have muddied the waters when it comes to properties that are rented through an agent or through an online facilitator such as Orbitz or Airbnb. If an accommodation is rented through such an online short-term rental (STR) platform, the owner of the property may not be liable for unpaid occupancy taxes on that rental. This is not a happy result for local tax collectors, because it almost certainly would be easier for a collector

---

221. The sales tax–related definitions found in G.S. 105-164.3 apply to local occupancy taxes. G.S. 105-164.3(35)a. defines "retailer" as "[a] person engaged in [the] business of making sales at retail." G.S. 105-164.3(36)d. defines the term "sales" to include a lease or rental. Therefore, any party in the business of leasing or renting out accommodations is a "retailer" for purposes of both sales and occupancy taxes.

222. G.S. 105-164.4F(a)(2).

223. G.S. 105-164.4F(a)(3).

to pursue enforced collection remedies against a local property owner rather than against an out-of-state online STR platform such as San Francisco–based Airbnb. The liability of these parties is discussed in the section immediately below.

B. Facilitator and Rental Agent Liability

The general statutory provisions addressing local occupancy taxes (G.S. 153A-155 (counties); 160A-215 (municipalities)) tie those taxes to G.S. 105-164.4F, the statute that governs sales taxes on the rental of accommodations. G.S. 105-164.4F makes the following statements about third-party rentals and their impact on retailers'[224] liability for occupancy taxes:

> "Facilitator Transactions. – . . . A facilitator that does not send the retailer the tax due on the sales price is liable for the amount of tax the facilitator fails to send. . . . *A retailer is not liable for tax due but not received from a facilitator.*"[225]
>
> "Rental Agent. – A person who, by written contract, agrees to be the rental agent for the provider of an accommodation is considered a retailer under this Article and is liable for the tax imposed by this section. *The liability of a rental agent for the tax imposed by this section relieves the provider of the accommodation from liability.*"[226]

Read together, these provisions lead to the conclusion that local tax collectors generally may not hold retailers responsible for occupancy taxes on rentals that are paid through real estate agents or brokers or through facilitators such as Airbnb, VRBO, or Orbitz *unless* the facilitator collects occupancy taxes on those rentals and remits them to the retailers.[227]

North Carolina appears to be in the minority of states that hold online facilitators—rather than individual property owners—responsible for occupancy taxes.[228] While the motivation behind this approach is not clear, it seems likely that

224. *Authors' Note*: The terms "retailer" and "provider" refer to the property owner of a rental accommodation.

225. G.S. 105-164.4F(c) (emphasis added).

226. G.S. 105-164.4F(d) (emphasis added).

227. This conclusion was confirmed by conversations with Ginny C. Upchurch, Director, Sales and Use Tax Division, N.C. Department of Revenue. As explained above, sales taxes on accommodations follow the same rules as local occupancy taxes.

228. A recent national tax survey concluded that of the thirty-nine states that levy taxes on short-term rentals, only fourteen hold facilitators responsible. The other twenty-five states hold property owners responsible for unpaid taxes on their rentals.

the North Carolina General Assembly assumed that the large companies running travel websites have deeper pockets than do local property owners. The legislature also may have also assumed that it is easier to collect a large tax payment from one taxpayer rather than to collect small tax payments from many individual taxpayers. While both of those assumptions sound reasonable, the end result is a bad one for local tax collectors, who have almost zero leverage over well-financed companies located outside of North Carolina.

Table 7 summarizes how and when each of the three different parties that may be involved in an accommodation rental (retailer, facilitator, and rental agent) are responsible for unpaid occupancy taxes.

Consider the example of Tommy Tar Heel, who owns a rental beach house in Dare County. Tommy might find himself in one of five possible occupancy tax liability scenarios:

1. If Tommy rents out the house himself, with no help from a rental agent or an online facilitator, then Tommy is of course responsible for collecting and paying the occupancy taxes owed on his beach house rentals. If the taxes are not paid in full, Tommy is responsible for the occupancy taxes and could be targeted with enforced collection remedies (see section VIII.D, *infra*, for more on these remedies).[229]
2. If Tommy lists his beach house on Airbnb but the tenant contracts directly with Tommy for the rental—meaning payment is made directly from the tenant to Tommy—then Tommy, and not Airbnb, is responsible for the occupancy taxes and could be targeted with enforced collection remedies.
3. If Tommy lists his beach house on Airbnb and the tenant contracts with Airbnb for the rental—meaning payment is made through that company's website—and Airbnb does not remit occupancy taxes on the rental to Tommy, then Airbnb is responsible for the occupancy taxes. The local government could target only Airbnb with enforced collection remedies.
4. If Tommy lists his beach house on Airbnb and the tenant contracts with Airbnb for the rental—meaning payment is made through that company's

Bloomberg Tax, Executive Summary: 2018 Survey of State Tax Departments, BNA.com, http://images.about.bna.com/Web/BloombergBNA/%7Bbae99449-382f-451a-9afa-3b45be3569b2%7D_TAX_WP_State-Tax-Survey-Summary_042418.pdf?utm_campaign=TAX_RPT_CONFIRM_2018%20State%20Tax%20Survey%20Summary_042618&utm_medium=email&utm_source=Eloqua&elqTrackId=46d395af324848d3bb592203882c9259&elq=380dc0ab65ad4f1c88aef594d769adae&elqaid=11087&elqat=1&elqCampaignId=8495.

229. G.S. 105-164.4(a)(3).

Table 7. Occupancy Taxes: Responsible Parties

This party is responsible for unpaid occupancy taxes . . .	If the following occurs:
Retailer (Property Owner)	No facilitator or rental agent is involved in the accommodation rental **OR** The accommodation is listed with a facilitator but the guest contracts with and pays the retailer directly for the accommodation rental **OR** The guest contracts with and pays the facilitator for the accommodation rental *and* the facilitator collects occupancy taxes from the guest and remits them to the retailer
Facilitator (Online STR Platform)	The guest contracts with and pays the facilitator for the accommodation rental *and* the facilitator does not collect occupancy taxes from the guest and remit them to the retailer
Rental Agent	The accommodation is listed with a rental agent

website—and Airbnb collects occupancy taxes from the tenant and remits them to Tommy, then Tommy, and not Airbnb, would be personally responsible for those taxes. Only Tommy could be targeted with enforced collection remedies for the taxes that were remitted to him.[230]

5. If Tommy contracts with a rental agent to rent out his beach house, then the rental agent, and not Tommy, is responsible for the occupancy taxes. If the occupancy taxes are not paid in full, then the local government could target the rental agent (but not Tommy) with enforced collection remedies. This remains true even if the rental agent lists the house on Airbnb or another online STR platform. The involvement of a facilitator does not appear to affect a rental agent's liability for occupancy taxes under G.S. 105-164.4F(d).

230. It is possible that both parties would be liable for a portion of the occupancy taxes. If Airbnb failed to collect and remit to Tommy the full amount of occupancy taxes on the rental, then Tommy would be responsible only for the amount of occupancy taxes remitted to him. Airbnb would be responsible for the shortfall.

1. Collection and Remittance of Occupancy Taxes by Certain Facilitators

The huge number—and turnover—of travel websites makes it impossible to know exactly how each one deals with occupancy taxes.[231] But knowing how a few of the major players in the field handle these taxes will help local tax collectors map out a strategy for maximizing occupancy tax revenues.

a. Airbnb

Airbnb, the world's most popular online STR platform for private residential accomodations, has seen its North Carolina revenues quadruple from $50 million in 2016 to $200 million in 2018. The company now lists more than 14,000 accommodations in North Carolina.[232]

Airbnb has been collecting occupancy taxes on North Carolina rentals and remitting those funds to local governments since it signed a tax agreement with the state Department of Revenue (DOR) in 2015.[233] Initial reports indicated that the agreement covered occupancy taxes in only four large North Carolina counties: Buncombe, Durham, Mecklenburg, and Wake.[234] While there is no indication that Airbnb has signed individual agreements with other North Carolina local governments, the company's website and anecdotal reports from local tax collectors suggest that Airbnb is now collecting and remitting local occupancy taxes directly to cities and counties all across North Carolina.[235] While the Airbnb agreement

---

231. *See* SimilarWeb, *Top Websites Ranking*, SIMILARWEB.COM, https://www.similarweb.com/top-websites/category/travel/accommodation-and-hotels (offering statistics on more than fifty travel websites).

232. Airbnb had the most web traffic of all online rental platforms as of December 2018. The company's growth in North Carolina has been documented in numerous media reports. *See, e.g.*, Mae Israel, UNC Charlotte Urban Institute, Div. of Academic Affairs, *Soaring Airbnb Rentals Make Mecklenburg County No. 2 in N.C.*, UNCC.EDU (Feb. 19, 2019), https://ui.uncc.edu/airbnb-clt; Hunter Ingram, *Airbnb Reports $13 million in 2018 New Hanover County Rentals*, STARNEWSONLINE (Wilmington) (Jan. 14, 2019), https://www.starnewsonline.com/news/20190114/airbnb-reports-13-million-in-2018-new-hanover-county-rentals; Cece Nunn, *Wilmington Outpaces Raleigh in Airbnb's Rankings for NC*, WILMINGTONBIZ.COM (Jan. 23, 2018), http://www.wilmingtonbiz.com/hospitality/2018/01/23/wilmington_outpaces_raleigh_in_airbnbs_rankings_for_nc/17038.

233. Taylor Knopf, *Airbnb to Collect and Pay Taxes in North Carolina*, NEWS & OBSERVER (Raleigh) (May 18, 2015), https://www.newsobserver.com/news/local/counties/wake-county/article21331905.html.

234. *Id.*

235. *See* Airbnb, *Occupancy Tax Collection and Remittance by Airbnb in North Carolina*, AIRBNB.COM, https://www.airbnb.com/help/article/2320/occupancy-tax-collection-and-remittance-by-airbnb-in-north-carolina. In this section of its website, Airbnb states as follows: "City and/or County Occupancy Tax: All locally imposed occupancy taxes will be collected on reservations in North Carolina. The tax varies by city and county. It is typically 1-8% of the listing price including any cleaning and guest

does help produce occupancy tax revenue for North Carolina's local governments, it suffers from the same concerns over secrecy and lack of transparency for which Airbnb's agreements with other states have been severely criticized.[236]

Because the DOR has refused to release details of its agreement with Airbnb, it is impossible to know exactly what obligations it creates on behalf of Airbnb concerning local occupancy taxes.[237] Local tax collectors in North Carolina report that Airbnb has been submitting monthly lump-sum occupancy tax payments that lack any details concerning the properties and rental dates to which the payments apply.[238] This lack of detail makes it essentially impossible to determine if the appropriate taxes have been paid on all accommodation rentals made through Airbnb. Local tax collectors have asked Airbnb for more information about the monthly payments, only to be ignored or told that Airbnb's agreement with the DOR does not require the company to identify the properties to which the payments relate.[239]

Airbnb's response lacks legal support. The authors are unaware of any statute that authorizes the DOR to waive a taxpayer's obligations for local taxes if the localities that levy those taxes are not parties to the agreement between the

---

fees for reservations less than 90 nights." In response to email queries from the authors, fifteen counties and towns across the state indicated that they are receiving monthly lump-sum occupancy taxes from Airbnb as of March 2019 (responses on file with authors).

236. Airbnb, *In What Areas Is Occupancy Tax Collection and Remittance by Airbnb Available?*, AIRBNB.COM, https://www.airbnb.com/help/article/653/in-what-areas-is-occupancy-tax-collection-and-remittance-by-airbnb-available (contains list showing that Airbnb has tax agreements with more than forty-five U.S. states and territories). Some industry observers find Airbnb's tax agreements problematic. *See, e.g.*, Paris Martineau, *Inside AirBnB's "Guerrilla War" Against Local Governments*, WIRED (Mar. 20, 2019), https://www.wired.com/story/inside-airbnbs-guerrilla-war-against-local-governments/; DAN R. BUCKS, AIRBNB AGREEMENTS WITH STATE AND LOCAL TAX AGENCIES: A FORMULA FOR UNDERMINING TAX FAIRNESS, TRANSPARENCY AND THE RULE OF LAW 2 (Mar. 2017), https://www.ahla.com/sites/default/files/Airbnb_Tax_Agreement_Report_0.pdf.

237. Multiple attempts by the authors to obtain from the DOR a copy of North Carolina's agreement with Airbnb were unsuccessful. Representatives from the DOR told the authors that this agreement was confidential tax information under G.S. 105-259. The authors disagree but were unwilling to take legal action to challenge the DOR's claim. The excessive confidentiality afforded the Airbnb contract with North Carolina is not unique. In Florida, a local tax collector was forced to sue her own state government in order to obtain a copy of the agreement between that state and Airbnb. Shortly after the lawsuit was filed, Florida turned over a copy of the Airbnb agreement to the local tax collector but demanded that she keep it confidential. Martineau, *supra* note 236.

238. As stated in numerous emails from local tax collectors to the authors in March 2019 (on file with authors).

239. *Id.*

taxpayer and the DOR. News reports and email responses to author queries of North Carolina local tax collectors suggest that only four of the state's 100 counties and none of the state's 500+ municipalities were party to the 2015 agreement with Airbnb.[240] It is unclear why Airbnb apparently has not pursued tax agreements with individual North Carolina local governments, as it has done in other states.[241] Absent such individual agreements, Airbnb should still be subject to the reporting and payment requirements for all North Carolina local occupancy taxes other than those in the four counties that signed the 2015 agreement.[242] While permitting Airbnb to collect and pay occupancy taxes without revealing the details behind those payments might be smart policy, that should be a decision for local officials to make for their own jurisdictions; it should not be decided by the DOR. The lack of transparency in Airbnb's agreement with North Carolina mirrors the experiences of other state and local governments across the country. A state tax expert who analyzed the publicly available tax agreements signed with Airbnb found that most prevented government officials from learning the names or addresses of Airbnb hosts.[243] As one Pennsylvania tourism industry official commented, when asked about a proposed agreement between Airbnb and one of that state's counties,

---

240. Knopf, *supra* note 233; March 2019 emails from local tax collectors to authors, *supra* note 238.

241. In May 2017, Airbnb claimed to have contracted with more than 275 local, state, and federal governments for the collection of taxes on accommodations in those jurisdictions. Airbnb Citizen, *Tax Agreements with 275 Governments*, AIRBNBCITIZEN.COM, https://www.airbnbcitizen.com/airbnb-tax-facts/. Media reports confirm that such contracts have been entered into at the local level in a variety of states. *See, e.g.*, Joe Rubino, *Airbnb to Take Over Denver Lodging Tax Collections from Hosts Starting April 1*, DENVER POST (Mar. 16, 2018), https://www.denverpost.com/2018/03/16/denver-airbnb-city-lodging-taxes/ (Colorado); Sara DiNatale, *Pinellas County Strikes Bed Tax Deal with VRBO, HomeAway and Other Airbnb Competitors*, TAMPA BAY TIMES (Sept. 19, 2018), https://www.tampabay.com/news/business/tourism/Pinellas-County-strikes-bed-tax-deal-with-VRBO-HomeAway-and-other-AirBnb-competitors-171940277 (Florida); Tracy Samilton, *Airbnb Strikes Hotel Tax Deal with Kent County*, MICHIGAN RADIO (July 18, 2018), http://www.michiganradio.org/post/airbnb-strikes-hotel-tax-deal-kent-county (Michigan); Veneta Rizvic, *Airbnb Reaches Tax Agreement with City of St. Louis*, ST. LOUIS BUSINESS JOURNAL (Nov. 14, 2018), https://www.bizjournals.com/stlouis/news/2018/11/14/airbnb-reaches-tax-agreement-with-city-of-st-louis.html (Missouri); Jason Jordan, *Airbnb Reaches Tax Deal with Steuben County*, Evening Tribune (Hornell) (Aug. 30, 2018), https://www.eveningtribune.com/news/20180830/strongairbnb-reaches-tax-deal-with-steuben-countystrong (New York); Bob Clark, *Airbnb, Allegany County Reach Tax Agreement*, OCEAN TIMES HERALD (Dec. 4, 2018), http://www.oleantimesherald.com/news/allegany_county/airbnb-allegany-county-reach-tax-agreement/article_aca8b5f6-f78a-11e8-bcc8-776e0d8fbe97.html (Pennsylvania).

242. Buncombe, Durham, Mecklenburg, and Wake counties apparently were parties to the 2015 agreement between Airbnb and the DOR. Knopf, *supra* note 233.

243. Martineau, *supra* note 236.

> What these agreements from Airbnb say, I refer to it as hush money. 'We'll write you a check every month. We're not going to give you any information to prove that this is the correct amount. We're not going to give you any information to show you who we're remitting on behalf of and you just leave us alone,' is essentially what these contracts say and it takes away any ability for the county to ensure that the correct amounts are being paid or for local governments to know where these [properties] are located.[244]

Airbnb fights hard to protect this "shield of secrecy" around the properties it lists, suing state and local governments that pass laws requiring travel websites to identify rental property addresses and changing the geocodes for its properties so that their latitudes and longitudes differ from their actual locations.[245]

Another concern about Airbnb's agreement with North Carolina is that permitting a facilitator such as Airbnb to send tax payments directly to the taxing governments violates G.S. 105-164.4F,[246] the statute that governs sales and occupancy taxes on accommodation rentals, by transferring liability from the property owner to the facilitator.[247] As discussed above, a local tax office would much prefer to use enforced collections remedies against a local property owner than against a California-based corporation with no assets in North Carolina.

---

244. Carter Walker, *Lancaster County Rejects Airbnb Voluntary Tax Collection Agreement; Critics Seek Level Playing Field*, LANCASTERONLINE (Apr. 9, 2018), https://lancasteronline.com/news/local/lancaster-county-rejects-airbnb-voluntary-tax-collection-agreement-critics-seek/article_69fc28b6-3a8c-11e8-ac3b-3328cfd2ac94.html (quoting Melissa Bova, Vice President of Government Affairs, Pennsylvania Restaurant and Lodging Association). According to this article, Lancaster County refused to sign Airbnb's proposed agreement.

245. Martineau, *supra* note 236.

246. G.S. 105-164.4F(c) states that a facilitator such as Airbnb "must send the retailer the portion of the sales price the facilitator owes the retailer and the tax due on the sales price no later than 10 days after the end of each calendar month." The statute does not contemplate the facilitator sending tax payments directly to the taxing government.

247. As discussed in the text above, the retailer (property owner) remains liable for occupancy taxes on rentals made through a facilitator only to the extent that the facilitator collects taxes on those rentals and remits those taxes to the retailer. If the facilitator sends those taxes directly to the taxing government, the retailer is no longer liable for underpayment of those taxes. G.S. 105-164.4F(c).

b. *Expedia, Orbitz, and Related Hotel-Reservation Websites*

The Expedia Group operates many of the major hotel-reservation websites, including Expedia, Hotels.com, Orbitz, and Travelocity.[248] According to most local tax officials with whom the authors have spoken, Expedia and related online hotel-reservation companies remit local occupancy taxes following the same approach as is used by Airbnb: each company provides monthly lump-sum occupancy tax payments to local governments without any supporting details as to which dates and which hotels the payments relate. However, at least one local government has had success obtaining additional details from Expedia. Officials in the town of Blowing Rock report that after a conversation with an Expedia official, that company and its related websites are now providing details along with their monthly occupancy tax payments that identify the specific hotels for which those payments were made and how much of each payment applies to each hotel.[249]

The authors could not find any evidence of a tax agreement between Expedia and any North Carolina governmental unit.[250] Although, like Airbnb, Expedia has signed agreements with some state and local governments,[251] it appears that in this state Expedia and its related websites are collecting and remitting state and local taxes directly to the taxing governments of their own accord. As is true with Airbnb, this (unofficial) practice violates the state statutory requirement that facilitators collect and remit accommodation taxes to property owners.[252] It also shifts responsibility for those taxes from property owners to Expedia.[253]

---

248. *See* Expedia Group, *Global Network of Brands*, ExpediaGroup.com, https://www.expediagroup.com/expedia-brands/. According to January 2019 web-traffic statistics, the Expedia Group owns six of the top ten most popular online travel websites. eBiz, *MBA Guide: Top 15 Most Popular Travel Websites*, eBizMBA.com (Jan. 2019), http://www.ebizmba.com/articles/travel-websites.

249. Email from Nicole Norman, Finance Director, Town of Blowing Rock, to the authors (Mar. 25, 2019) (on file with authors). Ms. Norman reported that Expedia began providing hotel details for its monthly payments shortly after the town contacted an Expedia official and requested that such information be provided. The town's occupancy tax form includes a "Schedule A" on which the taxpayer is expected to list the addresses of each accommodation for which occupancy tax payments are being made. Town of Blowing Rock, Occupancy Tax Form, http://www.townofblowingrocknc.gov/services/occupancy-tax-form.

250. None of the fifteen local governments that replied to the authors' March 2019 email inquiries reported that it had signed an agreement with Expedia or any of its subsidiaries. March 2019 emails from local tax collectors to authors, *supra* note 238.

251. *See, e.g.*, Veronica Brezina-Smith, *Pinellas Partners with TripAdvisor, Expedia to Collect Tourist Taxes*, Tampa Bay Business Journal (Sept. 19, 2018), https://www.bizjournals.com/tampabay/news/2018/09/19/pinellas-partners-with-tripadvisor-expedia-to.html

252. G.S. 105-164.4F(c).

253. *Id.*

Also similar to the way Airbnb operates is Expedia's usual failure to supply supporting details when it submits lump-sum payments to taxing governments. But there may be ways to overcome this problem. The first is to learn from Blowing Rock's experience and attempt to convince Expedia to provide additional detail along with its tax payments.[254] The second is to work directly with the hotels that list their rooms on Expedia. Expedia's travel websites are more well-known for booking hotel rooms than for renting private residences.[255] Local tax collectors report that hotels, especially the major chains, more often and more reliably report and pay occupancy taxes to local government than do owners of private residences. As part of hotels' monthly occupancy tax reporting process, local collectors can encourage/require each hotel to report not only rentals booked directly with the hotel but also those made through a facilitator such as Expedia or Orbitz.[256] This kind of reporting should give a local government some information as to the amount of occupancy taxes it should expect to receive from Expedia and other online facilitators. But because those facilitators collect taxes for so many hotels, the task of associating Expedia's monthly lump-sum payments with the hotels' monthly reporting remains daunting.

Expedia and its related websites have battled with many state and local governments over the correct sales price on which occupancy taxes should be applied.[257] The online companies prefer to apply state and local taxes only on the room price that a hotel charges the online company, while the government units believe that their taxes should be applied to the (higher) room price the online company charges the guest. In 2014, the General Assembly eliminated this controversy in North Carolina by amending the state's sales tax provisions (which also control occupancy

---

254. *See supra* note 249.

255. Although rentals of private residences are available on Orbitz, its homepage offers a link to hotel reservations but not to private residence rentals. *See* https://www.orbitz.com/. Roughly 40 percent of all online hotel reservations are made through an online travel agent (OTA) such as Expedia or Orbitz rather than directly through hotel websites. Eran Feinstein, *OTAs vs. Direct Hotel Bookings: Which Is the Leading Trend for 2018?*, TRAVELDAILYNEWS.COM (Feb. 23, 2018), https://www.traveldailynews.com/post/otas-vs-direct-hotel-bookings-which-is-the-leading-trend-for-2018.

256. Daniel McCarty, Wake County's appraisal and collection manager, reported that hotels submit monthly occupancy tax reports to taxing governments that include information on both rentals made directly with hotels (in such cases the hotels submit occupancy taxes) and those made through facilitators such as Orbitz (which are reported as "not subject to tax" because the facilitator has (hopefully) already collected and paid the taxes). Email from Daniel McCarty to authors (Jan. 10, 2019) (on file with authors).

257. *See* Paul Stinson, *Online Travel Companies Prevail in $84 Million Texas Tax Dispute*, DAILY TAX REPORT: STATE, BNA.COM (Nov. 30, 2017), https://www.bna.com/online-travel-companies-n73014472652/.

taxes) to make clear that the tax applies to the room price charged to the guest, not the discounted room price charged by the hotel to the online company.[258]

c. *Priceline and Related Hotel-Reservation Websites*

Priceline is owned by Bookings Holdings, which also operates the hotel-reservation sites Bookings.com and KAYAK.[259] Local tax officials report that they do not receive any payments from any of these sites. The Priceline website indicates that its hotels charge guests directly for all room costs and taxes.[260] Assuming this is true for all hotels listed on Priceline, then the hotels would be responsible for all occupancy taxes on the listed rentals because they were booked directly with the hotels and not with the online facilitator. However, if Priceline and its corporate siblings do charge some customers directly for hotel reservations, then the facilitator would be responsible for the occupancy taxes on those rentals.

d. *HomeAway*

Once an independent company, HomeAway was acquired by the Expedia Group in 2015.[261] The "HomeAway Family" serves as the parent company for several popular STR platforms, including VRBO.com and VacationRentals.com.[262] HomeAway allegedly collects state and local taxes and remits them directly to the taxing governments in at least ten states and Puerto Rico.[263] Unfortunately, North Carolina

---

258. S.L. 2014-3, Section 8.1(b) created a new statute, G.S. 105-164.4F. Subsection (b) of that statute states that "[t]he sales price of the rental of an accommodation marketed by a facilitator includes charges designated as facilitation fees and any other charges necessary to complete the rental." This language, along with similar verbiage in subsection (c) of the law, requires the facilitator to collect sales taxes (and, therefore, occupancy taxes) on the sales price paid by the guest to the facilitator, not on the (potentially lower) price that the retailer charges the facilitator for that room.

259. *See* Jonathan Vanian, *Why Priceline Group Is Changing its Name to Booking Holdings*, FORTUNE (Feb. 21, 2018), http://fortune.com/2018/02/21/priceline-group-booking-holdings/.

260. This is the language currently appearing on the Priceline website when a user clicks on the "taxes" portion of the estimated charge for a hotel room reservation: "Charges for Taxes and Service Fees: We will not charge you when you complete this transaction. You will be charged directly by the hotel for the 'Total Estimated Charges' shown below. Unless expressly stated, taxes and service fees are excluded from your room rate, and in addition to the 'Total Estimated Charges' shown below, you will be charged applicable taxes, including, without limitation, sales and use tax, occupancy tax, room tax, excise tax, value added tax and/or other similar taxes, by the hotel you select."

261. *See* Picker, *supra* note 22.

262. The full list of HomeAway-owned sites is found at https://www.homeaway.com/info/about-the-family.

263. *See* VRBO, *What Stay Taxes/Lodging Taxes Does Home Away Collect and Remit?*, VRBO.COM, https://help.vrbo.com/articles/What-Stay-Taxes-Lodging-Taxes-does-HomeAway-collect-and-remit.

Table 8. Occupancy Taxes—Responsible Party Based on Facilitator Approach

Facilitator/(Standard Occupancy Tax Practice)	Party Responsibility for Occupancy Tax
Airbnb (Monthly lump-sum payments made directly to taxing governments)	Airbnb
Expedia (Monthly lump-sum payments made directly to taxing governments)	Expedia
Priceline (Guests contract directly with hotels)[a]	Individual hotels
HomeAway (Taxes collected and paid to property owner if property owner adds tax charge to rental cost)	Property owner (for taxes collected and paid to property owner) *and/or* HomeAway (for taxes not collected from guests)

a. Exception: If a guest pays for a hotel reservation through Priceline, then Priceline, and not the hotel, would be responsible for the occupancy taxes on the rental unless Priceline collects those taxes and remits them to the hotel.

is not one of these states. Local tax collectors in our state report that they do not receive any tax payments directly from HomeAway.

Instead, property owners listing rentals in North Carolina (and in the other states in which HomeAway does not automatically collect state and local taxes) are permitted to add taxes to the cost of their rentals at whatever rates they choose.[264] Presumably, HomeAway forwards these tax charges to the property owners with the expectation that the owners will remit them to the appropriate taxing governments. If this is the case, then under G.S. 105-164.4F(c), responsibility for these taxes remains with the property owners and not with HomeAway.

e. Summary

Table 8 summarizes the responsibility for occupancy taxes under the different payment/remittal approaches normally used by the facilitators discussed in this section.

As Table 8 indicates, liability for occupancy taxes on rentals processed through the Airbnb and Expedia websites would transfer from the rental property owners to those facilitators under the companies' standard approaches to occupancy tax collection. However, local tax collectors should not assume that, once an accom-

264. *See* VRBO, *How Do I Add or Edit My Tax Rate?*, VRBO.COM,https://help.vrbo.com/articles/How-do-I-add-or-edit-my-tax-rate A search of North Carolina property listings on VRBO.com demonstrated that the tax charges included in rental price quotes varied greatly, from zero to 14 percent of the rental rate.

modation is listed on Airbnb or Expedia, the local government has no remedies against the property owner. Before concluding that those facilitators are the only parties responsible for occupancy taxes on all properties listed on their websites, tax collectors may demand evidence from local rental property owners that the rentals in question were processed by and paid for through a facilitator (see scenario 3 in the Tommy Tar Heel example in section VII.B, *supra*). If, instead, the guests contracted directly with the property owners, the property owners—and not Airbnb or Expedia—should be responsible for the related occupancy taxes (see scenario 2 in the Tommy Tar Heel example). If the property owners decline to produce evidence that Airbnb or Expedia received the rental payments, then it seems reasonable for the tax collector to proceed under the assumption that the property owners remain responsible for the occupancy taxes on those rentals.

Under Priceline's practice of having guests contract directly with the hotels listed on its site, responsibility for occupancy taxes remains with the hotels. But based on the authors' experimentation with the website, some Priceline hotel reservations appear to be paid through Priceline and not directly to the hotel. If Priceline does not collect and remit occupancy taxes on those reservations to the hotels, then Priceline would be responsible for occupancy taxes on those rentals rather than the hotels.

With respect to HomeAway rentals that include charges for state and local taxes, responsibility remains with the property owners because HomeAway apparently sends those tax collections directly to the property owners and not to the taxing governments. Property owners who fail to remit those taxes to the government may be held personally liable for those taxes. But if property owners listing on HomeAway websites choose not to add taxes to the rental price of their properties, then liability stays with HomeAway and not the property owners. This legal structure provides property owners with a perverse incentive *not* to include state and local taxes on rentals listed with online travel agents.

Under the HomeAway approach, it is also possible that liability for occupancy taxes is split between the online facilitator and the property owner. Assume that a North Carolina property owner lists her Dare County beach house on VRBO for a weekly rental of $1,000. The total charges include a tax charge of 5 percent, or $50, which the tenant pays and which VRBO remits to the property owner along with the principal rent amount of $1,000. The 5 percent tax charge is clearly not the appropriate total of state and local taxes that apply to the rental of an accommodation in Dare County. The county levies an occupancy tax of 6 percent.[265] State and

265. County of Dare, N.C., *Occupancy Tax*, DareNC.com, https://www.darenc.com/departments/tax-department/occupancy-tax.

local sales tax would add another 6.75 percent,[266] for a total state and local tax rate of 12.75 percent. The total tax collected on a $1,000 rental in Dare County should be $127.50 and not the $50 actually charged to the tenant via VRBO. Responsibility for the $127.50 is split between VRBO and the property owner. As a facilitator, VRBO is responsible for the $77.50 in taxes that were not collected and forwarded to the property owner. The property owner is responsible for the $50 in taxes that were collected and remitted to her by VRBO.

C. Penalties for Failure to Pay Occupancy Taxes

Unless a specific local occupancy tax bill calls for different penalties, the penalties applicable to late sales taxes also apply to late occupancy taxes, thanks to the uniform provisions for local occupancy taxes.[267] These penalties are (1) a 5-percent-per-month penalty for failure to file the required monthly return, up to a maximum of 25 percent[268] and (2) a one-time 10 percent penalty for failure to pay the tax along with the monthly return.[269] G.S. 105-236(a)(9) also makes the failure to file a return or pay the tax a Class 1 misdemeanor, which means a local government could pursue criminal prosecutions against delinquent occupancy taxpayers if its local law enforcement agency and district attorney agreed to cooperate.

1. Estimating Delinquent Occupancy Taxes

In most cases of delinquent occupancy taxes, the accommodation owner will not have submitted a return. How, then, may the taxing government determine the amount of tax and associated penalties that are owed? The best approach is simply to estimate the revenue that the accommodation owner likely received for renting out the accommodation during the relevant time period.

The tax office can find a comparable hotel or rental house and use that comparable rental rate to estimate the tax owed by the delinquent accommodation

---

266. This figure represents the regular 4.75 percent state sales tax rate and Dare County's 2 percent local option sales tax rate. *See Effective Dates of Local Sales and Use Tax Rates in North Carolina Counties*, FILESNC.GOV (as of Oct. 1, 2018), https://files.nc.gov/ncdor/documents/files/levydates_10-18.pdf.

267. G.S. 153A-155(e) (counties), 160A-215(e) (municipalities). Each provision incorporates the sales tax penalties found in G.S. 105-236. Although the property tax enforced collection remedies of attachment and garnishment and levy and sale are made applicable to occupancy taxes through G.S. 153A-147 (counties) and 160A-207 (municipalities), property tax interest under G.S. 105-360 does not apply to occupancy taxes.

268. G.S. 105-236(a)(3).

269. G.S. 105-236(a)(4).

Quiz: Penalties for Failure to Pay Occupancy Taxes

Question: If a hotel retailer neglected to file and pay $1,000 in occupancy tax for a particular month, what penalty would apply?

(a) $100

(b) $150

(c) $200

(d) $250

Answer: (b)—$50 for the failure to file (5 percent of $1,000) plus $100 (10 percent of $1,000) for the failure to pay.

owner for the relevant time period. The next step would be to create an estimated occupancy tax bill and mail it to the accommodation owner, informing the owner that he/she/it has some reasonable amount of time (perhaps thirty or sixty days) to appeal the estimated tax assessment and provide evidence of the correct amount. Property owners could also provide proof that their properties were rented through facilitators or agents who, as described above, might be liable for the occupancy taxes in question. That proof should include financial reports from the facilitators indicating whether occupancy taxes were collected and remitted to the property owners by the facilitators. If the accommodation owners fail to produce such proof, then the local government may move forward with enforced collection remedies (discussed in the next section) against those owners.

D. Enforced Collection Remedies

Like all local taxes, occupancy taxes may be collected using the property tax remedies of attachment and garnishment (for wages, bank accounts, and other funds owed to the taxpayer) and levy and sale of personal property (cars, boats, furniture, computers, etc.).[270] Unlike property taxes, however, occupancy taxes do not automatically create a lien on real property. As a result, a local government may not foreclose on real property to satisfy occupancy taxes unless it files a lawsuit in state court and obtains a judgment against the taxpayer.

270. G.S. 153A-147 (counties), 160A-207 (municipalities).

Quiz: Enforced Collection Remedies for Occupancy Taxes

Facts: Billy Blue Devil rents out his beach house in Duck, N.C., through Carolina Beach Vacations, Inc. (CBV), a local rental agency. CBV lists the house for rent on VRBO and Airbnb. Occupancy taxes have not been paid on any rentals for the 2018 summer season. Which of these collection remedies are available to the town to collect the delinquent occupancy taxes?

(a) Garnishment of Billy's wages
(b) Attachment of CBV's bank account
(c) Foreclosure on the beach house
(d) All of the above

Answer: (b). The rental agency is responsible for the delinquent taxes.

For more details on the property tax remedies of attachment and garnishment and levy and sale, see the School of Government's treatise on property tax collection.[271]

While these enforced collection remedies are extremely effective for taxpayers with assets in North Carolina,[272] they are less helpful against out-of-state taxpayers such as Airbnb or Expedia who have no assets in North Carolina. Local tax collectors seeking to enforce their rights against out-of-state delinquent taxpayers usually will be required to pursue litigation both in North Carolina and in the taxpayers' home states.[273] Depending on the amount of taxes involved, this effort may require more time and money than a local government is willing to invest.

---

271. Christopher B. McLaughlin, Fundamentals of Property Tax Collection Law in North Carolina (UNC School of Government 2012), available for purchase at https://www.sog.unc.edu/publications/books/fundamentals-property-tax-collection-law-north-carolina.

272. These same methods help North Carolina counties collect more than 99 percent of their owed property taxes. Aggregate collection rates for counties and municipalities are available on the State Treasurer of North Carolina's website (customizable form): https://www.nctreasurer.com/slg/lfm/financial-analysis/Pages/Analysis-by-Population.aspx.

273. Although a local tax collector does not need a court judgment to attach funds held by North Carolina banks, these "administrative" attachments are unlikely to be honored in other states. *See* Martin C. Brook, *Compliance Rules for Out-of-State Garnishments*, Nat'l L. Rev. (Mar. 9, 2017), https://www.natlawreview.com/article/compliance-rules-out-state-garnishments. As a result, a local tax collector seeking to collect delinquent taxes against a debtor's property in another state may need to obtain a court judgment against that debtor in a North Carolina court and then ask a court in the debtor's home state to honor that judgment under either the U.S. Constitution's Full Faith and Credit Clause, U.S. Const. art. IV, § 1, or under that state's version of the Uniform Enforcement of Foreign Judgments Act (UEFJA). *See generally* Uniform Law

E. No Successor Liability

Absent a special provision in a given local occupancy tax bill, there is no successor liability for occupancy taxes.[274] As a result, new owners of rental houses or hotels are not responsible for occupancy taxes owed by the old owners.[275]

For example, assume that ABC, Inc. owns a hotel in Blowing Rock, N.C., and is delinquent on two years of occupancy taxes. Before Watauga County begins enforced collection actions against ABC, Inc., the hotel is sold to XYZ, Inc. ABC, Inc. remains responsible for the delinquent occupancy taxes. XYZ, Inc. would be responsible for all occupancy taxes going forward, but it does not assume liability for the occupancy taxes that relate to the period during which ABC, Inc. owned the hotel. The county's only available remedies for those old delinquent occupancy taxes would be to use attachment and garnishment against ABC, Inc.'s bank accounts or other funds or to levy on and sell personal property owned by ABC, Inc. Because XYZ, Inc. is not responsible for occupancy taxes generated during ABC, Inc.'s ownership of the hotel, the county has no remedy against XYZ, Inc.'s bank accounts or its personal or real property (including the hotel that generated the delinquent occupancy taxes).

F. Best Practices for Improving Occupancy Tax Compliance

All local governments that levy occupancy taxes should consistently seek to educate accommodation owners about their obligations for these taxes. This education can take place through personal visits with major property owners or hotel operators, speeches at chamber of commerce meetings and similar local business events, advertising in local media, and direct mail and email campaigns. Local tax collectors believe, with reason, that the more their taxpayers learn about the

---

Commission, *Enforcement of Foreign Judgments Act*, UNIFORMLAWS.ORG, https://www.uniformlaws.org/committees/community-home?CommunityKey=e70884d0-db03-414d-b19a-f617bf3e25a3 (listing states that have enacted the UEFA from 1953 through 2019). See also North Carolina's UEFJA, G.S. Ch. 1C, Art. 17.

274. For example, Wake County's local bill, S.L. 1995-458, states that "[t]he provisions of Article 5 and Article 9 of Chapter 105 of the General Statutes apply to this act." Those articles in Chapter 105 include G.S. 105-164.38(b), which creates personal liability on the part of the buyer of a property or business that owes sales taxes. As a result, in Wake County the buyer of a property or business that owes occupancy taxes becomes liable for those occupancy taxes.

275. This differs from the rules that apply to delinquent property taxes on real property. The owner on the date of delinquency and all subsequent owners of the real property are responsible for those taxes. G.S. 105-365.1.

occupancy tax and the benefits provided by its revenues, the more likely they are to comply with their tax obligations.

After education, local tax collectors report that identification of accommodation rentals is the second most important step for increasing occupancy tax compliance. Some towns and counties assign staff members the job of searching all local accommodation listings on Airbnb, VRBO, HomeAway, and similar online STR platforms. These employees pull together as much information as can be culled from those listings, including address, owner contact information, rental history, and rates. The tax office then uses this information to reach out to the identified owners to remind them of their tax obligations and, if necessary, begin the tax estimation and enforcement process described above.

IX. Local Government Administration

The uniform provisions for occupancy taxes in G.S. 153A-155 and 160A-215 state that occupancy taxes are due on or before the 20th of each month for rental income earned in the previous month.[276] These provisions also state that the taxes are payable to the county or city finance officer, but most local governments assign occupancy tax collection duties to their property tax collectors. As is true with property tax collection, cities are free to contract with their counties (or vice-versa) for the collection of occupancy taxes.[277]

The uniform provisions permit local governments to develop their own occupancy tax returns. (See the links in the footnotes below for examples from Buncombe County[278] and Wake County.[279]) Note that neither of these return forms provide for a "retailer discount" referenced in the last sentence of G.S. 105-155(c).[280]

---

276. G.S. 153A-155(d), 160A-215(d).

277. For more on interlocal tax collection agreements, see Chris McLaughlin, *Interlocal Agreements for Property Tax Collection*, Coates' Canons: NC Loc. Gov't L. blog (Nov. 30, 2018), https://canons.sog.unc.edu/interlocal-agreements-for-property-tax-collection/.

278. Buncombe Cty. Gov't, Buncombe Cty. Occupancy Tax Monthly Remittance Form, https://www.buncombecounty.org/common/tax/monthly-remittance-form.pdf.

279. Wake Cty. Revenue Dep't, Room Occupancy Tax Div., Wake Cty. Room Occupancy Tax Return, http://www.wakegov.com/tax/business/Documents/Gross%20Recs%20Forms/ROT%20Coupon2018.pdf.

280. The provision states, "An operator of a business who collects a room occupancy tax may deduct from the amount remitted to the taxing city a discount equal to the discount the State allows the retailer for State sales and use tax."

Because North Carolina does not currently offer retailers a discount on state sales taxes, there should be no retailer discount for occupancy taxes under this provision.[281]

Most local occupancy tax bills allow local governments to retain a certain percentage of occupancy tax revenue to cover the administrative cost of collecting the tax before they remit the remainder of the revenue to Tourism Development Authorities (TDAs), entities that will spend the revenue in support of local tourism and other permitted uses.[282] (TDAs are discussed in more detail in section X, *infra*.) The General Assembly normally limits this collection-cost percentage to 3 percent of the first $500,000 of gross occupancy tax proceeds, plus 1 percent of all proceeds above $500,000.[283]

Using these percentages, if a city were to gross $800,000 per year in occupancy taxes, it would be entitled to keep $18,000 for administrative costs ((3 percent × 500,000) + (1 percent × 300,000)). The remaining $782,000 would be transferred to the city's TDA.

As is true with all occupancy tax issues, local governments should refer to their local bills for the collection percentages applicable to their occupancy taxes.

A. Refunds and Retroactive Billing

None of the uniform occupancy tax provisions or local occupancy tax bills create guidelines for how local governments should deal with situations involving the over- or under-assessment of occupancy taxes. The fact that property tax enforced collection remedies may be used for the collection of occupancy taxes[284] does not mean that the property tax rules concerning overpayments and underpayments apply to occupancy taxes. As a result, local governments are free to develop their own rules concerning refunds of occupancy tax overpayments by taxpayers or the retroactive billing of occupancy taxes that were under-assessed or never assessed in prior years.

---

281. The current sales and use tax return required by the North Carolina Department of Revenue contains no reference to a retailer discount. *See* N.C. DEP'T OF REVENUE, SALES & USE TAX RETURN, https://files.nc.gov/ncdor/documents/forms/e500_10-14_webfill.pdf. Nor do the statutes that reference a retailer's sales tax collection and remittance obligations. *See* G.S. 105-164.7, -164.8.

282. See, for example, Section 1(c)(1) of the Caswell County/Yanceyville occupancy tax bill, S.L. 2007-224.

283. LEGISLATIVE GUIDELINES, cited in full *supra* note 186.

284. As discussed above, property tax attachment and garnishment remedies and levy and sale remedies are available for all local taxes pursuant to G.S. 153A-147 (counties) and 160A-207 (municipalities).

Local governments could choose to follow the rules for property taxes, which generally limit refunds and retroactive assessments to five years.[285] Or they could follow the state sales tax and income tax provisions, which generally limit refunds and retroactive assessments to three years.[286] Or they could develop their own unique rules. Regardless of the approach chosen, a local government should create objective, written policies regarding over- and under-assessments of occupancy taxes. These policies should be well publicized to both tax officials and taxpayers to increase the likelihood of consistent application and decrease the likelihood of surprises.

Refunds of occupancy taxes made to property owners, facilitators, or rental agents should be forwarded by those parties to the tenants who originally paid the refunded taxes. A local government has no obligation to ensure that this occurs. But state sales tax refund provisions allow the state to refuse to make a sales tax refund unless the retailer receiving the refund credits the purchaser who originally paid the tax.[287] Local governments could institute a similar rule for refunds of overpayments of occupancy taxes.

B. Public Access to Occupancy Tax Payment Records

As discussed in detail section X.D, *infra*, occupancy tax returns are confidential.[288] So, too, are occupancy tax payment records relating to individual taxpayers, as these records could reveal those taxpayers' incomes.[289] Local governments should not disclose occupancy tax payment information to parties who are not involved with the administration of the occupancy tax.

---

285. G.S. 105-380 and -381 create the rules for local governments to provide refunds or releases (waivers) in certain cases of over-assessment and/or overpayment of property taxes. G.S. 105-312 (discovery) and -394 (immaterial irregularity) create the rules for local governments to pursue taxes that were not assessed at the correct amount or not assessed at all.

286. G.S. 105-241.6(a) (refunds), -241.8(a) (assessments).

287. G.S. 105-164.11(a)(1).

288. G.S. 153A-155(d).

289. G.S. 153A-148.1, 160A-208.1.

X. Tourism Development Authorities

The typical local occupancy tax bill requires the taxing jurisdiction to create a tourism development authority (TDA) to control the spending of local occupancy tax proceeds. The local governing board—city council or county commissioners—levy the occupancy tax, but the TDA decides how to spend the proceeds of that tax.

A TDA's structure and the specifics of its expenditure authority can vary from jurisdiction to jurisdiction. But the General Assembly's occupancy tax guidelines call for a board with the following make-up: at least one-half of board members must be "currently active in the promotion of travel and tourism in the taxing district" and at least one-third must be "affiliated with organizations that collect the tax," in other words, people who work in the hospitality industry or who own rental properties.[290] Many local occupancy tax bills contain language similar to this excerpt from the Caswell County and Yanceyville local occupancy tax bill:

> Tourism Development Authority.—(a) Appointment and Membership.— When the Board of Commissioners adopts a resolution levying a room occupancy tax under this act, it shall also adopt a resolution creating the Caswell County Tourism Development Authority, which shall be a public authority under the Local Government Budget and Fiscal Control Act. The resolution shall provide for the membership of the Authority, including the members' terms of office, and for the filling of vacancies on the Authority. At least one-third of the members shall be individuals who are affiliated with businesses that collect the tax in the county, and at least one-half of the members shall be individuals who are currently active in the promotion of travel and tourism in the county. The Board of Commissioners shall designate one member of the Authority as chair and shall determine the compensation, if any, to be paid to members of the Authority.[291]

As is true of the Caswell County/Yanceyville bill, most local occupancy tax bills allow the local governing board (meaning board of county commissioners or city council) the discretion to determine the size of the TDA board and the term length for its members. Members of the governing board are permitted to serve as TDA members, so long as the overall membership of the TDA satisfies the statutory

290. *See* LEGISLATIVE GUIDELINES, *supra* note 186.
291. S.L. 2007-224.

requirements and the governing board members do not violate the statutory limits on holding multiple offices.[292]

What options does a local governing board have if it is unhappy with its TDA board?[293] Clearly, the governing board can choose not to reappoint one or more TDA board members at the end of their terms for any reason. But local governing boards are more limited if they wish to remove TDA members in the middle of their terms.

Neither the General Assembly's *Guidelines for Occupancy Tax Legislation* (*Legislative Guidelines*)[294] nor the typical local occupancy tax bill discusses how and when TDA board members may be removed. However, the North Carolina courts have concluded that if a law provides that a person is appointed to a government office for a set term, that person may be removed only for cause and after notice and the opportunity for a hearing.[295] Because TDA members must be appointed for set terms, they are protected by this "for cause" removal requirement in the middle of their terms. "Cause" in this context generally means a serious criminal offense (in other words, a felony) or misconduct relating to the office.[296] It almost

---

292. Current North Carolina law generally limits any one person to one elective and one appointive office, or two appointive offices, at the same time. G.S. 128-1.1. For a more detailed discussion of this issue, including whether *ex officio* appointments count toward this limit, see Fleming Bell, *Wearing Several Hats: Multiple and Ex Officio Office-Holding*, Coates' Canons: NC Loc. Gov't L. blog (Apr. 20, 2010), https://canons.sog.unc.edu/wearing-several-hats-multiple-and-ex-officio-office-holding/.

293. The motivation for removing a TDA member might also come from the TDA itself. *See, e.g.*, Becky Johnson, *TDA Wants Reece Off Board*, Smoky Mountain News (Mar. 1, 2006), https://www.smokymountainnews.com/news/item/13815-tda-wants-reece-off-board (discussing Haywood County, N.C., TDA's call for removal of one of its board members). As this article suggests, the TDA board has no authority to remove one of its own members. If such authority exists, it is held by the local governing board. The Haywood County issue became moot when the TDA board member in question passed away a few months after the TDA asked for his removal. *See* Becky Johnson, *Reece's Larger-Than-Life Personality Will Be Missed, Say Friends*, Smoky Mountain News (June 28, 2006), https://smokymountainnews.com/news/item/13318-reece-s-larger-than-life-presence-will-be-missed-say-friends.

294. Cited in full *supra* note 186 and reproduced in Appendix B.

295. *Stephens v. Dowell*, 208 N.C. 555 (1935). For a more complete discussion of this issue, see Frayda Bluestein, *Removing Members of Appointed Boards*, Coates' Canons: NC Loc. Gov't L. blog (June 3, 2015), https://canons.sog.unc.edu/removing-members-of-appointed-boards/.

296. See, for example, the limitations on removing members of local public health boards (G.S. 130A-35(g)), local consolidated human services boards (G.S. 153A-77(c)), and local community college boards of trustees (G.S. 115D-19). Removal from these boards requires a finding of certain misconduct on the part of the board member in question, including commission of a felony, conflicts of interest, habitual failure to attend meetings, or "conduct that tends to bring the office into disrepute."

certainly does not include a TDA board member's refusal to comply with the policy preferences of the city council or board of county commissioners.[297] If policy disagreements are the only reason a governing board wants to get rid of certain TDA board members, removal will need to wait until the terms of those TDA board members end.

A. Spending Occupancy Tax Proceeds: Two Primary Permitted Uses

Local occupancy tax bills specify the purposes for which occupancy tax proceeds may be spent by the TDA. Typically, these funds may not be used for a local government's general operations.[298] Instead, nearly all local occupancy tax bills require that the proceeds be spent to "promote travel and tourism" (two-thirds of net tax proceeds) or for "tourism-related expenditures" (one-third).[299]

In its *Legislative Guidelines*, the General Assembly defines the promotion of travel and tourism as "costs associated with advertising and marketing an area or tourist activity. These expenditures include the cost to conduct market research, publish promotional materials, or engage in similar promotional activities to attract tourists."[300] That same document defines tourism-related expenditures as those that are "anticipated to increase the use of lodging facilities, meeting facilities and convention centers by attracting tourists or business travelers to the area. Tourism-related expenditures may include capital expenditures."[301]

Because the definitions of "promotion of tourism" and "tourism-related" are somewhat subjective, there is no bright-line rule to determine when an expendi-

---

297. For appointed boards whose existence is not required by law, local governing boards can rely on a much more radical solution to policy differences: they may abolish the existing board and appoint new members to a new version of the board. But because TDAs are required to be created by local occupancy tax authorization bills, they are not optional and, thus, the "nuclear" option of disbanding the entire TDA board is not available. *See Bd. of Adjustment of Swansboro v. Town of Swansboro*, 334 N.C. 421 (1993).

298. Two counties, Cleveland and Hyde, may use their occupancy tax revenue for any lawful purpose. Hyde County, however, must spend a specific percentage of that revenue to benefit certain portions of the county. S.L. 1989-173 (Cleveland County), S.L. 1991-806 (Hyde County).

299. *See* Legislative Guidelines, *supra* note 186.

300. *Id.*

301. *Id. See also* Magellan Strategy Group, Profile of North Carolina Occupancy Taxes and Their Allocation 9 (version 4.1, Apr. 2017), https://www.ncrla.org/wp-content/uploads/2017/10/2017_NC-Occupancy-Tax-Profil-1.pdf (Caswell Beach, Holden Beach, Ocean Isle Beach, and Sunset Beach all classify "tourism-related expenditures" as including items such as "the criminal justice system, fire protection, public facilities and utilities, . . . and waste and sewage treatment control . . .").

ture satisfies one of these two primary permitted uses. The authors are unaware of any North Carolina cases in which a TDA expenditure was the subject of a legal challenge, meaning there are no court opinions to help local governments apply the definitions provided by the General Assembly. So long as a TDA can provide a reasonable explanation of how a particular expenditure would promote tourism or is related to tourism, it seems likely that the expenditure would be found to satisfy the occupancy tax restrictions. That said, the question of classifying an expenditure will no doubt be more of a political—rather than a legal—one, since local elected boards have appointment power over the TDAs that make occupancy tax spending decisions.

Examples of occupancy tax expenditures that would likely fall under either the "promotion of tourism" or the "tourism-related" category include

- advertising the town, county, or region in travel magazines or websites;
- constructing or maintaining a visitor's bureau or a convention center;
- developing youth, amateur, or professional sports facilities that generate substantial hotel activity;
- funding ocean rescue and beach patrol programs;
- installing new or additional signage relating to area tourist attractions;
- maintaining public restroom facilities in tourist areas;
- promoting arts or sporting events in the area that directly impact tourism and hotel activity; and
- restoring or preserving historical properties that attract tourists.

Other spending decisions may be more difficult to analyze than the ones set out in the bulleted list above. Consider the following debatable expenditures.

1. A donation of $1,000 to the local chamber of commerce for its annual fundraiser dinner.

   Occupancy tax proceeds can be shared with a local chamber of commerce to help fund its efforts to advertise local businesses across the state. But using occupancy tax funds to support a dinner that will be attended primarily by local residents and business owners seems questionable. The legality of an occupancy tax–funded donation in support of a chamber of commerce should turn on whether the tax funds will be used to attract tourists (permitted) or to encourage local residents to patronize local businesses (probably not permitted).

2. A donation by one county to a neighboring county to help promote a music festival in that adjacent county that will attract out-of-town artists and music enthusiasts.

It seems reasonable for one jurisdiction to use its occupancy tax revenues to help promote an event in a neighboring jurisdiction if it can reasonably be assumed that the jurisdiction donating the funds will also see a boost in tourism from the event. For example, the town of Atlantic Beach could spend its occupancy tax funds to promote the N.C. Aquarium a few miles down Route 58 in Pine Knoll Shores. But a decision by Atlantic Beach to spend its occupancy tax funds to promote the Battleship North Carolina, located 100 miles away in Wilmington, would be on shakier legal ground.

3. Paying for the construction of additional lighting, sidewalks, or landscaping in a downtown business district.

   Assuming the downtown district contains shops and attractions targeting tourist dollars, it seems acceptable to spend occupancy tax funds on improvements that will make the district even more attractive to tourists. In contrast, lighting and streetscape improvements for a traditional office park would a questionable use of occupancy tax funds. Such improvements may make the office park more attractive to other businesses, but it seems unlikely to attract tourists to the area.

B. Spending Occupancy Tax Proceeds: Additional Permitted Uses

As noted in section X.A, *supra*, while most local occupancy tax bills limit a TDA's use of occupancy tax proceeds to "promotion of tourism" and "tourism-related expenses," there are many examples of additional permitted uses across the state. The most common additional permitted use is beach nourishment, for which most of the state's coastal counties and municipalities have received authority to allocate up to one-half of their occupancy tax proceeds.[302] Other permitted uses across the state include promoting "industrial and economic growth,"[303] financing convention

---

302. See for example, S.L. 2001-381, permitting Carteret County to use up to 50 percent of its occupancy tax funds for beach nourishment. That bill defines the term "beach nourishment" by using the definition promulgated in the General Assembly's *Legislative Guidelines*: "The placement of sand, from other sand sources, on a beach or dune by mechanical means and other associated activities that are in conformity with the North Carolina Coastal Management Program along the shorelines of the Atlantic Ocean of North Carolina and connecting inlets for the purpose of widening the beach to benefit public recreational use and mitigating damage and erosion from storms to inland property."

303. *See, e.g.*, S.L. 1987-472 (Caswell County).

Quiz: Permitted Occupancy Tax Spending Uses

Question: Which of these expenditures is likely an unauthorized use of occupancy tax funds?

(a) Funding additional police protection during a local craft beer festival

(b) Erecting new signage that advertises local businesses along the interstate highway that runs through the region

(c) Purchasing advertisements that promote the area in Our State and similar North Carolina–centric magazines

(d) Construction of a new elementary school

Answer: (d). While new schools may encourage people to move to an area, they are unlikely to help promote tourism in the area.

centers,[304] operating theaters and art spaces,[305] constructing the NASCAR Hall of Fame,[306] funding criminal justice systems,[307] and providing solid waste and sewer treatment services.[308] The one use of occupancy tax funds that appears to be off-limits is for the construction of a hotel, which is prohibited by the uniform occupancy tax guidelines in G.S. 153A-155(f1) and 160A-215(f1)—although the General Assembly could avoid this restriction through the use of a local bill if it so desired.

C. Borrowing Money

In addition to spending limitations, TDAs also face limitations on borrowing money. A TDA has no authority by itself to borrow money. This restriction results from a state constitutional prohibition against the General Assembly conferring the authority to borrow money in a local act.[309] Because all TDAs are created via local acts, they may not be granted the authority to borrow money.[310]

---

304. Numerous local governments have financed convention or civic centers using occupancy tax proceeds, including Pitt County, S.L. 1993-410.

305. *See, e.g.*, S.L. 2012-144 (Henderson County).

306. *See, e.g.*, S.L. 2005-68 (Mecklenburg County).

307. *See, e.g.*, S.L. 1991-154 (covering several local governments, including the town of Rowland).

308. *See, e.g.*, S.L. 1991-664 (covering several local governments, including the village of Bald Head Island).

309. N.C. Const. art. V, § 4(1).

310. For more on this issue, please see Kara Millonzi, *May a Tourism Development Authority (TDA) Borrow Money?*, Coates' Canons: NC Loc. Gov't L. blog (Dec 21,

Several local acts state that a TDA may expend occupancy tax proceeds "to finance" the building of a facility. In the context of a TDA (which is constitutionally barred from borrowing money), the term "to finance" must be interpreted to mean "to fund" or "pay for" and not "to borrow."

Although a TDA may not itself borrow funds, it may become indirectly involved in a borrowing transaction initiated by a city or county. G.S. 160A-461 provides that any unit of local government, which includes a TDA, may contract with one or more other units of local government to execute any undertaking that all of the parties to the contract are statutorily authorized to undertake. Most TDAs are permitted to spend occupancy tax funds on capital projects relating to tourism (see the standard definition of "tourism-related expenditures" discussed above.) This authority would allow the TDA to enter into an intergovernmental agreement with its city or county to jointly fund a capital project that will attract tourists, such as a convention center, theater, or sports venue. The city or county could commit to borrow the funds necessary to front the costs of the project, and the TDA could commit to make yearly appropriations of occupancy tax revenue to the local government to cover some or all of the loan payments.

This approach has at least one major limitation, at least from the perspective of the local government that contracts with the TDA for such a capital project. Although the Local Government Budget and Fiscal Control Act authorizes a TDA to enter into a binding, multi-year contract,[311] the TDA can only commit money that it actually receives. If a TDA does not receive sufficient occupancy tax in any given year to cover the payment promised to the local government to help pay the capital loan, the local government will be on the hook for the shortfall.

D. TDA Access to Occupancy Tax Payment Records

Local governments and TDA board members may be surprised to learn that a TDA has no legal right to see occupancy tax returns or payment records for individual taxpayers. The uniform provisions for occupancy taxes in G.S. 153A-155 and 160A-215 state that occupancy tax returns are not public records and may be disclosed only as permitted by G.S. 153A-148.1 and 160A-208.1.[312] The latter two statutes govern the release of records containing income information and describe the very limited circumstances under which such records may be released. Occupancy tax records are considered to contain income information because if one knows how

---

2015), https://canons.sog.unc.edu/may-a-tourism-development-authority-tda-borrow-money/.

311. G.S. 159-13.

312. G.S. 153A-155(d), 160A-215(d).

Quiz: Occupancy Tax Records: TDA Access

Question: To which occupancy tax records should a TDA board have access?

(a) Tax payment totals for all hotels in the jurisdiction, in the aggregate

(b) A list of all hotels that have paid occupancy taxes in the past year

(c) A list of all hotels that owe occupancy taxes for the past year

(d) All of the above

Answer: (d). Records that show tax payments or tax obligations for individual taxpayers are confidential. But lists of taxpayers and total amounts paid in the aggregate by different types of taxpayers (e.g., hotels or private residence owners) are a matter of public record and may be disclosed to a TDA or to the general public.

much occupancy tax is owed or paid by a taxpayer, one can use that information, plus the jurisdiction's tax rate, to calculate the income earned by that taxpayer for the period in question.

Of the roughly half-dozen justifications for releasing income information outside the tax office described in G.S. 153A-148.1 and 160A-208.1, the only one that might apply to a TDA is this one: "to sort, process, or deliver tax information on behalf of the county, as necessary to administer a tax."[313] However, a TDA is not involved in "administering" the occupancy tax—it does not levy or collect occupancy taxes. That is the role of the local government. A TDA's only role is to spend occupancy tax funds in accordance with the restrictions created by a relevant local bill. Because TDAs do not administer the occupancy tax, this exception does not apply to TDAs. Nor do any of the other exceptions in G.S. 153A-148.1 and 160A-208.1.

As a result, a TDA has the same right as does the general public to see occupancy tax returns or payments records, which is to say a TDA has *no* right to see that information. If a town or the county were to release occupancy tax returns or payments records to a TDA, it would violate North Carolina public records laws.

TDA board members—and members of the general public—do have the right to see aggregate occupancy tax payment records. Records that summarize the total amount of occupancy tax paid by all taxpayers or by some general subset of taxpayers (e.g., hotels vs. private homes, all on-line travel agents) in a jurisdiction would be public in nature and subject to disclosure to a TDA or third parties.[314]

313. G.S. 53A-148.1(a)(3), 160A-208.1(a)(3).

314. Local governments must take care not to release occupancy tax information that could be easily tied to a particular taxpayer and that taxpayer's income. For example, if a town had only a single hotel in its jurisdiction but many rental homes, the town should not break out occupancy tax revenue into "hotel" and "private home" categories because

So, too, would be lists of all property owners that have paid or that owe property taxes, so long as those lists do not include tax amounts paid or owed by each property owner. But a TDA should not have access to any payment records for specific property owners, facilitators (e.g., Airbnb and other online travel agents), or rental agents.

In contrast, because local governing boards—county commissioners and municipal councils—are the entities that levy and oversee the administration of occupancy taxes, those boards may have access to payment records for individual taxpayers. Governing boards who have access to such payment information have an obligation not to disclose it to third parties, including TDAs.

---

the hotel tax payment total could be used to calculate the income of the town's lone hotel.

Appendix A. Model Short-Term Rental Ordinance

Disclaimer: The provisions contained in the model ordinance illustrate the regulatory concepts discussed in this publication. Each local government should consult with its attorney and other local officials to draft an STR ordinance that is both responsive to specific community needs and consistent with state and local law.

Section 1: Purpose.

WHEREAS, Section 160A-385 of the North Carolina General Statutes authorizes local governments to amend ordinances regulating land use within their jurisdiction.

WHEREAS, the purpose of this ordinance is to regulate short-term rentals (STRs), with the following goals recommended as key to preserving the health, safety, and general welfare of Town Citizens, protection of neighborhoods and property values:

1. To clearly define short-term rental.
2. To clearly identify where short-term rentals are permitted.
3. To establish basic safety regulations for visitors renting short-term properties.
4. To protect neighborhoods from unwanted short-term rentals and the problems that arise as a result (parties, noise, parking, dogs, trash, etc.).
5. To have a local contact to quickly and effectively address issues that may arise during a rental stay.
6. To allow homeowners the opportunity to legally rent their dwelling units where permitted.
7. To regulate short-term rentals consistent with authority given by the North Carolina General Statutes.

Section 2: Scope of Article.

The provisions of the section shall apply to whole-house short-term rentals. This section does not apply to other types of transient lodging, such as hotels, motels, homestays, or bed and breakfast establishments.

Except as provided in this section, nothing herein shall be construed to prohibit, limit, or otherwise supersede existing local authority to regulate the short-term rental of property through general land use and zoning authority. Nothing in this section shall be construed to supersede or limit contracts or agreements between or among individuals or private entities related to the use of real property.

Section 3: Definitions.

Code Compliance Verification Form is a document to be executed by a short-term rental owner to certify that the property complies with applicable zoning, building, health, and life safety code provisions.

Designated Responsible Party is the local contact person responsible for responding to complaints or issues stemming from the use of the dwelling unit as a short-term rental.

Homestay is the rental, for a period not to exceed thirty (30) consecutive days, of a room or rooms within a private residence for compensation while the permanent resident resides on-site during the duration of the rental period.

Hosting Platform means an online platform that allows property owners to advertise a dwelling unit as a short-term rental and facilitates the booking transaction for accommodations between a short-term rental owner and short-term rental guest, including, but not limited to, reservations and/or collection of payment for such accommodations on behalf of the short-term rental owner.

Incidental Vacation Rental is the listing of or rental of a residential dwelling unit for fewer than fourteen (14) days per year. If a dwelling unit is made available as a short-term rental for more than 14 days per year, the owner is responsible for obtaining a short-term rental permit even if the property ends up being rented for fewer than fourteen (14) days.

Whole-House Short-Term Rental ("STR" or "short-term rental") means the rental or lease of an attached or detached residential dwelling unit to guests for a duration not to exceed thirty (30) consecutive days.

Guest means the person(s) renting a residential dwelling unit for compensation for fewer than thirty (30) consecutive days.

Operator means the owner of, or any natural person, company, or rental agency who advertises, the property for rent and/or who otherwise facilitates the use of the property as a short-term rental.

Owner means the owner of record of the short-term rental property as recorded in the ______ County Land Records Office. The owner may be a natural person, or any form of business entity recognized by the State of North Carolina. If the owner is a form of business entity, the business entity shall maintain current registration with the North Carolina Secretary of State.

Short-Term Rental Zoning Permit ("STR permit") is the authorization required to use the property as a whole-house short-term rental upon registration. The short-term rental zoning permit shall include a registration number. No person shall rent, lease, or otherwise exchange for compensation any portion of a dwelling unit intended for use as short-term rental without first registering the property and securing a short-term rental zoning permit.

Section 4: Application Process.

A. Terms of STR Permit

1. Short-term rentals are hereby recognized as an appropriate land use. STRs are a permitted use within the following zoning districts: [*Local government to list all applicable districts.*]
2. An STR permit shall be assigned to each residential dwelling unit used as a short-term rental. STR permits shall be valid for one year from the date issued. STR permits shall automatically expire unless the owner submits a renewal application prior to expiration. The owner may apply for a renewal within sixty (60) days before expiration.
3. On or after _________, it shall be a violation of the Town's Unified Development Ordinance (UDO) to operate a short-term rental without having secured a valid STR permit.
4. Applications for STR permits shall be submitted with supporting documents and fees to the Planning Department via delivery or U.S. Mail.
5. An STR permit shall be obtained for each dwelling unit that is to be rented for a period of fewer than thirty (30) consecutive days.
6. For purposes of this ordinance, authorized applicants are referred to as "owners" and are those persons authorized in Section(s) ______ of the UDO to submit applications for zoning, special use, conditional use, or sign permits.
7. In the event of a sale or other transfer of any residential dwelling unit holding a valid STR permit, the permit shall automatically expire.

8. There is no requirement that a property owner must apply for an STR permit for incidental vacation rentals.

B. Application Process

(a) *Application.* In order to obtain an STR permit, the property owner shall submit an application along with the required supporting documentation and non-refundable application fee. The application shall contain the following information:

1. Name and contact information of the property owner, including telephone number, mailing address, and email address. If the owner is a corporation, firm, partnership, association, organization, or other group acting as a unit, the owner shall provide the name of the entity set forth exactly as shown in its articles of incorporation; the mailing address, telephone number, and email address of an individual who is the entity's statutory agent, president, or managing individual; the state in which the entity is incorporated or registered; and the entity's incorporation/registration number;
2. The address of the residential dwelling unit to be used as a short-term rental;
3. The addresses of all short-term rental properties located within the planning jurisdiction for which the property owner already holds a valid STR permit;
4. The name, address, telephone number, and email address of a designated responsible party for the short-term rental, which shall constitute his or her 24-hour contact information;
5. A site-plan showing the number of bedrooms and the location of the on-site improved parking area; and
6. A signed acknowledgment of the maximum occupancy requirements for short-term rental properties.

(b) *Supplemental Documentation.* Attached to and concurrent with the submission of the application described in this section, the property owner shall provide:

1. A sworn Code Compliance Verification Form;
2. Proof of general liability insurance indicating that the dwelling unit is used as a short-term rental;
3. Proof that the property owner is authorized to use the dwelling unit as a short-term rental. This shall include a copy of one of the following issued in the owner's name: (a) the deed to the property, (b) a recent mortgage

statement (issued within the previous two months), or (c) the previous year's property tax assessment; and

4. Proof of notification to property owners within 100 feet of the STR that the residential dwelling will be used as a short-term rental. Proof of notification is to be provided in the form of a Certificate of Mailing. This is a certification by the United States Postal Service that a letter was mailed. The receipt for the certificate shall be stapled to a copy of the notification that was submitted to nearby property owners. The notification shall include:
   a. Street address of proposed short-term rental;
   b. A statement that the property owner is applying for an STR permit.
   c. Name and contact information for the owner;
   d. Name and contact information for the designated responsible party, if different from the owner; and
   e. Maximum allowable occupancy for the property.

(c) *Grounds for Denial.* An application for an STR permit may be denied if any of the following has occurred:

a. The property owner submitted an incomplete application,
b. The proposed short-term rental fails to meet a specified standard, or
c. A renewal applicant has incurred more than three (3) verified violations of this section during the preceding twelve (12) months.

The property owner may appeal the denial of an STR permit to the Board of Adjustment in accordance with the provisions set forth in Article ___, Section ___ of the UDO. Owners have thirty (30) days from the date the denial was issued to appeal.

Section 5: Operational Requirements.

The following operational requirements apply to all short-term rental properties:

(1) Maximum Overnight Occupancy. The overnight occupancy of an STR shall not exceed two (2) guests per bedroom plus two (2) additional guests. The maximum number of guests in a short-term rental is limited to [X number of] guests, excluding children under three (3) years of age. Bedrooms used in calculating occupancy shall be taken from the permit application as affirmed by the property owner. For homes on a conditional or non-standard septic system, the maximum overnight occupancy shall be equal to the design load of the septic system. The occupancy limit shall be posted prominently within the short-term rental unit. The owner shall

ensure that all online listings and advertisements clearly set forth the maximum number of overnight guests permitted.

(2) Events. Special events, including weddings, receptions, and large gatherings, are not permitted in STRs. Owners of properties that have an overnight capacity of greater than [X number of] guests, or owners who seek to advertise and use a dwelling unit for large events, are required to apply for a special use permit with the Board of Adjustment.

(3) Display of Registration Number. Owners must prominently display the registration number in all online STR advertisements.

(4) Designated Responsible Party. All STRs operating within this planning jurisdiction shall have a designated responsible party who is available twenty-four hours a day during all times that the property is rented or used on a transient basis. The name, telephone number, and email address of the designee shall be conspicuously posted within the short-term rental unit. The designee shall reside within twenty (20) miles of the short-term rental property and be available to respond to complaints within forty-five (45) minutes of their receipt. A designee's repeated failure to timely respond to complaints may result in the revocation of the STR permit.

(5) Noise. The amount of noise generated by the STR use shall not disrupt the activities of the adjacent landowners.

(6) Trash and Recycling Disposal. The dates and instructions for trash and recycling collection shall be posted prominently within the STR. Trash receptacles must be the size and number authorized by existing refuse contracts. The STR operator shall ensure that all receptacles are set out for collection on the proper collection day and removed from the street or alley on the scheduled collection day, in accordance with Section ____ of the Code.

(7) Parking. The owner shall provide adequate on-site parking, to include a minimum of one (1) parking spot for every two (2) bedrooms on an improved parking surface. No recreational vehicles, buses, or trailers shall be parked on the adjoining street or visible on the property in conjunction with the short-term rental use.

(8) Age Requirements. The principal guest of a short-term rental unit shall be at least twenty-one (21) years old.

(9) Minimum Duration. The property owner shall not make the residential dwelling unit available to short-term rental guests for a period of less than overnight.

(10) The simultaneous rental to more than one party under separate contracts shall be prohibited.

(11) Food. The STR operator shall not prepare food for guests or provide pre-packaged or unpacked food items or beverages to guests.

Section 6: Miscellaneous Requirements.

1. Records. A short-term rental owner shall retain a log book dating back three (3) years and, upon request, make it available to the local tax office. The log shall include the dates of rental periods and the nightly rate charged during each night of a rental stay.
2. Advertisements. All advertisements or rental listings on online hosting platforms shall include the following information:
   a. Maximum occupancy requirement,
   b. On-site parking availability, and
   c. STR registration number.
3. Taxes. Short-term rental owners are responsible for paying the state sales tax, personal property taxes, and the transient occupancy tax as established by state and local law.
4. Inspections. [*Local government to determine whether to require safety inspections or self-inspection checklist.*]

Section 7: Enforcement and Review.

1. Enforcement. The procedures for the enforcement of this ordinance are set forth in Article ___, Section(s) _____ of the UDO.
2. Penalties and Remedies for Violations. The penalties and remedies for violations of this ordinance are set forth in Article ___, Section(s) _____ of the UDO.
3. Permit Revocations. The procedures for STR permit revocations, including the appeals process, are set forth in Article ___, Section(s) ___ of the UDO.
4. Operating Without a Permit. Any person who is found to be operating a short-term rental property without having been issued an STR permit shall be in violation of Article ___, Section ___ of the UDO.
5. Action for Recovery of Civil Penalty. If payment of a civil penalty is not made, or if violations are not cured or corrected, within the time specified in the citation, then the matter may be referred to the city attorney for institution of a civil action before a court of competent jurisdiction.

Appendix B. Guidelines for Occupancy Tax Legislation

Since 1983, the General Assembly has authorized many units of local government to levy a room occupancy tax. In several instances, the General Assembly has authorized both a county and a city within that county to impose an occupancy tax. The rate of tax, the use of the tax proceeds, the administration of the tax, and the body with the authority to determine how the tax proceeds will be spent vary considerably.

Over the past several years, there has been a greater effort to make the occupancy taxes uniform. In 1997, the General Assembly enacted uniform municipal and county administrative provisions for occupancy tax legislation—G.S. 153A-155 and G.S. 160A-215. These provisions provide uniformity in the areas of levy, administration, collection, repeal, and penalties.

The North Carolina Travel and Tourism Coalition (NCTTC) has a policy statement for legislation authorizing local occupancy taxes. Many of the principles contained in its statement are similar to the ones established by the House Finance Committee in 1993. Subsequently, the House Finance Committee established the Occupancy Tax Subcommittee, which regularly reviews occupancy tax legislation and looks for the inclusion of the following uniform provisions in the bills it considers:

Rate—The county tax rate cannot exceed 6% and the city tax rate, when combined with the county rate, cannot exceed 6%.

Use—At least two-thirds of the proceeds must be used to promote travel and tourism and the remainder must be used for tourism-related expenditures, which may include beach nourishment. However, local governments in coastal counties may allocate up to 50% of occupancy tax proceeds for beach nourishment, so long as all remaining proceeds are used for tourism promotion and provided that the use of occupancy tax proceeds for beach nourishment is limited by either a statutory cap or sunset provision.[315]

---

315. In May 2013, the North Carolina Travel and Tourism Coalition passed a resolution supporting a modification to the *Occupancy Tax Guidelines* to allow local governments in coastal counties to allocate up to 50 percent of occupancy tax proceeds for beach nourishment, so long as all remaining proceeds are used for tourism

Definitions—The terms "net proceeds", "promote travel and tourism", "tourism-related expenditures", and "beach nourishment" are defined terms:

Net proceeds—Gross proceeds less the costs to the city/county of administering and collecting the tax, as determined by the finance officer, not to exceed 3% of the first $500,000 of gross proceeds collected each year and 1% of the remaining gross receipts collected each year.

Promote travel and tourism—To advertise or market an area or activity, publish and distribute pamphlets and other materials, conduct market research, or engage in similar promotional activities that attract tourists or business travelers to the area; the term includes administrative expenses incurred in engaging in these activities.

Tourism-related expenditures—Expenditures that, in the judgment of the Tourism Development Authority, are designed to increase the use of lodging facilities, meeting facilities, and convention facilities in a city/county by attracting tourists or business travelers to the city/county. The term includes tourism-related capital expenditures.

Beach Nourishment[316]—The placement of sand, from other sand sources, on a beach or dune by mechanical means and other associated activities that are in conformity with the North Carolina Coastal Management Program along the North Carolina shorelines and connecting inlets for the purpose of widening the beach to benefit public recreational use and mitigating damage and erosion from storms to inland property. The term includes expenditures for the following:

a. Costs directly associated with qualifying for projects either contracted through the U.S. Army Corps of Engineers or otherwise permitted by all appropriate federal and State agencies;

promotion and provided that the use of occupancy tax proceeds for beach nourishment is limited by either a statutory cap or sunset provision.

316. During the 2001 Regular Session, the Occupancy Tax Subcommittee of the House Finance Committee considered several bills authorizing the use occupancy tax proceeds for beach nourishment. Although "beach nourishment" was not among the uses contained in the uniform guidelines, the subcommittee nevertheless concluded that beach nourishment was an acceptable expansion of the occupancy tax use provisions. In doing so, the subcommittee drafted this uniform definition of beach nourishment for use in occupancy tax legislation.

b. The nonfederal share of the cost required to construct these projects;
c. The costs associated with providing enhanced public beach access; and
d. The costs of associated nonhardening activities such as the planting of vegetation, the building of dunes, and the placement of sand fences.

Administration—The net revenues must be administered by a local tourism promotion agency, typically referred to as a "Tourism Development Authority," that has the authority to determine how the tax proceeds will be used, is created by a local ordinance, and at least ½ of the members must be currently active in the promotion of travel and tourism in the taxing district and ⅓ of the members must be affiliated with organizations that collect the tax.[317]

Costs of Collection—The taxing authority may retain from the revenues its actual costs of collection, not to exceed 3% of the first $500,000 collected each year plus 1% of the remainder collected each year.

Conformity with Other Local Occupancy Taxes—In 2008, the NCTTC formally revised its policy position with regard to occupancy taxes to include a statement that if a city seeks to impose a new occupancy tax or increase its existing tax on lodging facilities in a county that also has an existing occupancy tax, the county occupancy tax must conform to the guidelines in order for the Coalition to support the proposed municipal tax. During the 2009 Regular Session, the House Finance Chairs[318] considered the revised policy statement of the NCTTC but declined to amend the House Finance Committee's Guidelines for Occupancy Tax accordingly.

Research Division
N.C. General Assembly
Revised 9/3/2013

317. In March 2005, the House Finance chairs decided to change the percentage of members that must be currently active in the promotion of travel and tourism from three-fourths to one-half. The House Finance chairs in 2005–06 were Representatives Alexander, Gibson, Howard, Luebke, McComas, and Wainwright.

318. During the 2009–2010 Session, the House Finance chairs were Representatives Luebke, Wainwright, Weiss, and Gibson.

Appendix C. Select North Carolina Occupancy Tax Statutes

[*All provisions are from the North Carolina General Statutes as of May 2019.*]

§ 105-164.4F. Accommodation rentals.

(a) Definition. – The following definitions apply in this section:

(1) Accommodation. – A hotel room, a motel room, a residence, a cottage, or a similar lodging facility for occupancy by an individual.

(2) Facilitator. – A person who is not a rental agent and who contracts with a provider of an accommodation to market the accommodation and to accept payment from the consumer for the accommodation.

(3) Rental agent. – The term includes a real estate broker, as defined in G.S. 93A-2.

(b) Tax. – The gross receipts derived from the rental of an accommodation are taxed at the general rate set in G.S. 105-164.4. Gross receipts derived from the rental of an accommodation include the sales price of the rental of the accommodation. The sales price of the rental of an accommodation is determined as if the rental were a rental of tangible personal property. The sales price of the rental of an accommodation marketed by a facilitator includes charges designated as facilitation fees and any other charges necessary to complete the rental.

(c) Facilitator Transactions. – A facilitator must report to the retailer with whom it has a contract the sales price a consumer pays to the facilitator for an accommodation rental marketed by the facilitator. A retailer must notify a facilitator when an accommodation rental marketed by the facilitator is completed, and the facilitator must send the retailer the portion of the sales price the facilitator owes the retailer and the tax due on the sales price no later than 10 days after the end of each calendar month. A facilitator that does not send the retailer the tax due on the sales price is liable for the amount of tax the facilitator fails to send. A facilitator is not liable for tax sent to a retailer but not remitted by the retailer to the Secretary. Tax payments received by a retailer from a facilitator are held in trust by the retailer for remittance to the Secretary. A retailer that receives a tax payment from a facilitator must remit the amount received to the Secretary. A retailer is not liable for tax due but not received from a facilitator.

The requirements imposed by this section on a retailer and a facilitator are considered terms of the contract between the retailer and the facilitator.

(d) Rental Agent. – A person who, by written contract, agrees to be the rental agent for the provider of an accommodation is considered a retailer under this Article and is liable for the tax imposed by this section. The liability of a rental agent for the tax imposed by this section relieves the provider of the accommodation from liability.

(e) Exemptions. – The tax imposed by this section does not apply to the following:

(1) A private residence, cottage, or similar accommodation that is rented for fewer than 15 days in a calendar year other than a private residence, cottage, or similar accommodation listed with a real estate broker or agent.

(2) An accommodation supplied to the same person for a period of 90 or more continuous days.

(3) An accommodation arranged or provided to a person by a school, camp, or similar entity where a tuition or fee is charged to the person for enrollment in the school, camp, or similar entity.

§ 153A-155. Uniform provisions for room occupancy taxes.

(a) Scope. – This section applies only to counties the General Assembly has authorized to levy room occupancy taxes.

(b) Levy. – A room occupancy tax may be levied only by resolution, after not less than 10 days' public notice and after a public hearing held pursuant thereto. A room occupancy tax shall become effective on the date specified in the resolution levying the tax. That date must be the first day of a calendar month, however, and may not be earlier than the first day of the second month after the date the resolution is adopted.

(c) Collection. – A retailer who is required to remit to the Department of Revenue the State sales tax imposed by G.S. 105-164.4(a)(3) on accommodations is required to remit a room occupancy tax to the taxing county on and after the effective date of the levy of the room occupancy tax. The room occupancy tax applies to the same gross receipts as the State sales tax on accommodations and is calculated in the same manner as that tax. A rental agent or a facilitator, as defined in G.S. 105-164.4F, has the same responsibility and liability under the room occupancy tax as the rental agent or facilitator has under the State sales tax on accommodations.

If a taxable accommodation is furnished as part of a package, the bundled transaction provisions in G.S. 105-164.4D apply in determining the sales price of the taxable accommodation. If those provisions do not address the type of package offered, the person offering the package may determine an allocated price for each item in the package based on a reasonable allocation of revenue that is supported by the person's business records kept in the ordinary course of business and calculate tax on the allocated price of the taxable accommodation.

A retailer must separately state the room occupancy tax. Room occupancy taxes paid to a retailer are held in trust for and on account of the taxing county.

The taxing county shall design and furnish to all appropriate businesses and persons in the county the necessary forms for filing returns and instructions to ensure the full collection of the tax. A retailer who collects a room occupancy tax may deduct from the amount remitted to the taxing county a discount equal to the discount the State allows the retailer for State sales and use tax.

(d) Administration. – The taxing county shall administer a room occupancy tax it levies. A room occupancy tax is due and payable to the county finance officer in monthly installments on or before the 20th day of the month following the month in which the tax accrues. Every person, firm, corporation, or association liable for the tax shall, on or before the 20th day of each month, prepare and render a return on a form prescribed by the taxing county. The return shall state the total gross receipts derived in the preceding month from rentals upon which the tax is levied. A room occupancy tax return filed with the county finance officer is not a public record and may not be disclosed except in accordance with G.S. 153A-148.1 or G.S. 160A-208.1.

(e) Penalties. – A person, firm, corporation, or association who fails or refuses to file a room occupancy tax return or pay a room occupancy tax as required by law is subject to the civil and criminal penalties set by G.S. 105-236 for failure to pay or file a return for State sales and use taxes. The governing board of the taxing county has the same authority to waive the penalties for a room occupancy tax that the Secretary of Revenue has to waive the penalties for State sales and use taxes.

(f) Repeal or Reduction. – A room occupancy tax levied by a county may be repealed or reduced by a resolution adopted by the governing body of the county. Repeal or reduction of a room occupancy tax shall become effective on the first day of a month and may not become effective until the end of the fiscal year in which the resolution was adopted. Repeal or reduction of a room occupancy tax does not affect a liability for a tax that was attached before the effective date of the repeal or reduction, nor does it affect a right to a refund of a tax that accrued before the effective date of the repeal or reduction.

(f1) Use. – The proceeds of a room occupancy tax shall not be used for development or construction of a hotel or another transient lodging facility.

(g) Applicability. – Subsection (c) of this section applies to all counties and county districts that levy an occupancy tax. To the extent subsection (c) conflicts with any provision of a local act, subsection (c) supersedes that provision. The remainder of this section applies only to Alleghany, Anson, Brunswick, Buncombe, Burke, Cabarrus, Camden, Carteret, Caswell, Chatham, Cherokee, Chowan, Clay, Craven, Cumberland, Currituck, Dare, Davie, Duplin, Durham, Edgecombe, Forsyth, Franklin, Graham, Granville, Halifax, Haywood, Henderson, Jackson, Madison, Martin, McDowell, Montgomery, Moore, Nash, New Hanover, Northampton, Pasquotank, Pender, Perquimans, Person, Randolph, Richmond, Rockingham, Rowan, Rutherford, Sampson, Scotland, Stanly, Swain, Transylvania, Tyrrell, Vance, Washington, Wayne, and Wilson Counties, to Harnett County District H, New Hanover County District U, Surry County District S, Watauga County District U, Wilkes County District K, Yadkin County District Y, and the Township of Averasboro in Harnett County and the Ocracoke Township Taxing District.

§ 160A-215. Uniform provisions for room occupancy taxes.

(a) Scope. – This section applies only to municipalities the General Assembly has authorized to levy room occupancy taxes. For the purpose of this section, the term "city" means a municipality.

(b) Levy. – A room occupancy tax may be levied only by resolution, after not less than 10 days' public notice and after a public hearing held pursuant thereto. A room occupancy tax shall become effective on the date specified in the resolution levying the tax. That date must be the first day of a calendar month, however, and may not be earlier than the first day of the second month after the date the resolution is adopted.

(c) Collection. – A retailer who is required to remit to the Department of Revenue the State sales tax imposed by G.S. 105-164.4(a)(3) on accommodations is required to remit a room occupancy tax to the taxing city on and after the effective date of the levy of the room occupancy tax. The room occupancy tax applies to the same gross receipts as the State sales tax on accommodations and is calculated in the same manner as that tax. A rental agent or a facilitator, as defined in G.S. 105-164.4F, has the same responsibility and liability under the room occupancy tax as the rental agent or facilitator has under the State sales tax on accommodations.

If a taxable accommodation is furnished as part of a package, the bundled transaction provisions in G.S. 105-164.4D apply in determining the sales price of the taxable accommodation. If those provisions do not address the type of package offered, the person offering the package may determine an allocated price for each item in the package based on a reasonable allocation of revenue that is supported by the person's business records kept in the ordinary course of business and calculate tax on the allocated price of the taxable accommodation.

A retailer must separately state the room occupancy tax. Room occupancy taxes paid to a retailer are held in trust for and on account of the taxing city.

The taxing city shall design and furnish to all appropriate businesses and persons in the city the necessary forms for filing returns and instructions to ensure the full collection of the tax. An operator of a business who collects a room occupancy tax may deduct from the amount remitted to the taxing city a discount equal to the discount the State allows the retailer for State sales and use tax.

(d) Administration. – The taxing city shall administer a room occupancy tax it levies. A room occupancy tax is due and payable to the city finance officer in monthly installments on or before the 20th day of the month following the month in which the tax accrues. Every person, firm, corporation, or association liable for the tax shall, on or before the 20th day of each month, prepare and render a return on a form prescribed by the taxing city. The return shall state the total gross receipts derived in the preceding month from rentals upon which the tax is levied. A room occupancy tax return filed with the city finance officer is not a public record and may not be disclosed except in accordance with G.S. 153A-148.1 or G.S. 160A-208.1.

(e) Penalties. – A person, firm, corporation, or association who fails or refuses to file a room occupancy tax return or pay a room occupancy tax as required by law is subject to the civil and criminal penalties set by G.S. 105-236 for failure to pay or file a return for State sales and use taxes. The governing board of the taxing city has the same authority to waive the penalties for a room occupancy tax that the Secretary of Revenue has to waive the penalties for State sales and use taxes.

(f) Repeal or Reduction. – A room occupancy tax levied by a city may be repealed or reduced by a resolution adopted by the governing body of the city. Repeal or reduction of a room occupancy tax shall become effective on the first day of a month and may not become effective until the end of the fiscal year in which the resolution was adopted. Repeal or reduction of a room occupancy tax does not affect a liability for a tax that was attached before the effective date of the repeal or reduction, nor does it affect a right to a refund of a tax that accrued before the effective date of the repeal or reduction.

(f1) Use. – The proceeds of a room occupancy tax shall not be used for development or construction of a hotel or another transient lodging facility.

(g) Applicability. – Subsection (c) of this section applies to all cities that levy an occupancy tax. To the extent subsection (c) conflicts with any provision of a local act, subsection (c) supersedes that provision. The remainder of this section applies only to Beech Mountain District W, to the Cities of Belmont, Conover, Eden, Elizabeth City, Gastonia, Goldsboro, Greensboro, Hickory, High Point, Jacksonville, Kings Mountain, Lake Santeetlah, Lenoir, Lexington, Lincolnton, Lowell, Lumberton, Monroe, Mount Airy, Mount Holly, Reidsville, Roanoke Rapids, Salisbury, Sanford, Shelby, Statesville, Washington, and Wilmington, to the Towns of Ahoskie, Beech Mountain, Benson, Bermuda Run, Blowing Rock, Boiling Springs, Boone, Burgaw, Carolina Beach, Carrboro, Cooleemee, Cramerton, Dallas, Dobson, Elkin, Fontana Dam, Franklin, Grover, Hillsborough, Jonesville, Kenly, Kure Beach, Leland, McAdenville, Mocksville, Mooresville, Murfreesboro, North Topsail Beach, Pembroke, Pilot Mountain, Ranlo, Robbinsville, Selma, Smithfield, St. Pauls, Swansboro, Troutman, Tryon, West Jefferson, Wilkesboro, Wrightsville Beach, Yadkinville, Yanceyville, to the municipalities in Avery and Brunswick Counties, and to Saluda District D.

Appendix D. Occupancy Tax Rates for North Carolina Counties and Select Municipalities, Fiscal Year (FY) 2016–2017

County	Rate (%)	Municipality	Rate (%)
Alamance	3%		
Alleghany	6%		
Anson	6%		
Ashe	3%	Town of West Jefferson	3%
Avery		Town of Banner Elk	6%
		Town of Beech Mountain	6%
		Town of Seven Devils	6%
		Town of Sugar Mountain	6%
Beaufort		Town of Washington	6%
Brunswick	1%	City of Southport	3%
(does not apply in Village of Bald Head Island)		Town of Caswell Beach	5%
		Town of Holden Beach	5%
		Town of Leland	3%
		Town of Oak Island	5%
		Town of Ocean Isle Beach	5%
		Town of Shallotte	3%
		Town of Sunset Beach	5%
		Village of Bald Head Island	6%
Buncombe	6%		
Burke	6%		

County	Rate (%)		Municipality	Rate (%)
Cabarrus	6%			
Caldwell	3%		City of Lenoir	3%
Camden	6%			
Carteret	6%			
Catawba			City of Claremont	4%
			City of Hickory	6%
Chatham	3%			
Cherokee	4%			
Chowan	5%			
Clay	3%			
Cleveland	3%		City of Kings Mountain	3%
			City of Shelby	3%
			Town of Boiling Springs	3%
			Town of Grover	3%
Columbus	3%			
Craven	6%			
Cumberland	6%			
Currituck	6%			
Dare	6%			
Davidson			City of High Point	3%
			City of Lexington	6%
			City of Thomasville	6%

County	Rate (%)	Municipality	Rate (%)
Davie	3%	Town of Bermuda Run	3%
		Town of Mocksville	3%
Duplin	6%		
Durham	6%		
Edgecombe	6%		
Forsyth	6%		
		Town of Kernersville	3%
Franklin	6%		
Gaston	3%	City of Belmont	3%
		City of Gastonia	3%
		City of Kings Mountain	3%
		City of Mount Holly	3%
Graham	3%	Town of Fontana Dam	3%
		Town of Robbinsville	3%
Granville	6%		
Guilford	3%	City of Greensboro	3%
		City of High Point	3%
		Town of Kernersville	3%
Halifax	5%	City of Roanoke Rapids	1%
Harnett *(excluding Dunn/ Averasboro area)*	6%	City of Dunn	6%
Haywood	4%		

County	Rate (%)		Municipality	Rate (%)
Henderson	5%			
Hertford	3%		Town of Ahoskie	3%
Hyde	3%			
Iredell			City of Statesville	5%
			Town of Mooresville	4%
Jackson	4%			
Johnston	3%		Town of Benson	2%
			Town of Kenly	2%
			Town of Selma	2%
			Town of Smithfield	2%
Lee	3%			
Lenoir	3%		City of Kinston	3%
Lincoln	3%		City of Lincolnton	3%
Macon	3%		Town of Franklin	3%
Madison	5%			
Martin	6%			
McDowell	5%			
Mecklenburg	8%			
Mitchell	3%			

County	Rate (%)	Municipality	Rate (%)
Montgomery	3%		
Moore	3%		
Nash	5%		
New Hanover	3%	City of Wilmington	3%
(plus additional 3% in unincorporated areas)		Town of Carolina Beach	3%
		Town of Kure Beach	3%
		Town of Wrightsville Beach	3%
Northampton	6%		
Onslow	3%	City of Jacksonville	3%
		Town of North Topsail Beach	3%
		Town of Surf City	3%
		Town of Swansboro	3%
Orange	3%	Town of Carrboro	3%
		Town of Chapel Hill	3%
		Town of Hillsborough	3%
Pamlico		Town of Oriental	3%
Pasquotank	6%		
Pender	3%	Town of Burgaw	3%
		Town of Surf City	3%
		Town of Topsail Beach	3%
Perquimans	6%		
Person	6%		
Pitt	6%		
Polk	3%	Town of Columbus	3%
		Town of Tryon	3%

County	Rate (%)	Municipality	Rate (%)
Randolph	5%		
Richmond	3%		
Robeson		City of Lumberton	6%
		Town of Pembroke	3%
		Town of Rowland	2%
		Town of St Pauls	6%
Rockingham	3%	City of Eden	2%
		City of Reidsville	2%
Rowan	3%	City of Salisbury	3%
Rutherford	6%		
Sampson	3%		
Scotland	6%		
Stanly	6%		
Surry (Unincorporated Areas Only)	6%	City of Mount Airy	6%
		Town of Dobson	6%
		Town of Elkin	6%
		Town of Pilot Mountain	6%
Swain	4%		
Transylvania	5%		
Tyrrell	6%		
Union		City of Monroe	5%
Vance	6%		

County	Rate (%)		Municipality	Rate (%)
Wake	6%			
Washington	6%			
Watauga	6%	C	Town of Beech Mountain	6%
(unincorporated areas only)			Town of Blowing Rock	6%
			Town of Boone	6%
			Town of Seven Devils	6%
Wayne	1%		City of Goldsboro	5%
Wilkes			Town of Elkin	6%
			Town of Wilkesboro	3%
Wilson	6%			
Yadkin	6%		Town of Jonesville	6%
(unincorporated areas only)			Town of Yadkinville	6%
Yancey	3%			

www.ingramcontent.com/pod-product-compliance
Lightning Source LLC
Chambersburg PA
CBHW081508200326
41518CB00015B/2425
* 9 7 8 1 5 6 0 1 1 9 5 0 0 *